Your Sales Management Guru's Guide to:

Leading High-Performance Sales Teams

"Ken Thoreson has hit a home run the *Your Sales Management Guru's Guide* series. If you want to take your sales team to the next level, read these books!" - **Jeb Blount, CEO of SalesGravy.com and Author of *People Buy You: The Real Secret to What Matters Most in Business* and *Power Principles***

"If you're a crazy-busy sales manager and constantly worried about reaching your revenue goals, follow Ken Thoreson's savvy advice to create a high-performance sales organization." - **Jill Konrath, Author of *SNAP Selling and Selling to Big Companies***

"Your Sale Management Guru's Guide is the most practical how-to book on the topic of recruiting top sales talent that I've read." - **Roberto (Bob) F. Sanchez, Managing Partner, SunGard Consulting Services and former CEO & Managing Partner of Sales Performance   International**

"Ken's series of books are jammed packed with processes, systems and ideas that can be easily implemented for immediate impact."- **Brett Clay, Author of *Selling Change: 101+ Secrets for Growing Sales by Leading Change***

"No fluff, no theory, no cheerleading, just substance. In his series of *Your Sales Management Guru's Guide* books, Ken Thoreson delivers solid, practical, actionable guidance for sales management success. From crafting a vision to maximizing the productivity of weekly sales meetings, Ken provides concrete recommendations that sales executives can begin applying immediately to make a positive difference in their teams' performance. " - **Tom Pick, Social Media Consultant and** *Webbiquity* **blog author.**

"Ken Thoreson's Your Sales Management Guru's books are among the best sales management books I have read." - **Thomas J.   Winninger, CPAE, founder of the Winninger Institute for Market Growth Strategies.**

"Quick, ready-to-use sales management tools that are right on target for today's new 21st Century sales environment. Now more than ever, sales leadership and sales management are critical components to organizational success. Effectively executing that role is essential. These tools are an invaluable asset to anyone who has responsibility for organizational sales success." - **Frank Chamberlain, International Sales Consultant and Trainer, President of Resource Technologies, Inc.**

"Ken Thoreson applies his in-depth experience to help sales leaders do the things which need to be done - consistently and persistently. If you are serious about becoming the very best sales leader that you possibly can become, I urge you to read Ken Thoreson's words of wisdom – and then read them again." - **Jonathan Farrington, CEO of Top Sales Associates, Chairman of The jf Corporation and the creator of Top Sales World.**

Your Sales Management Guru's Guide to:

Leading High-Performance Sales Teams

by Ken Thoreson

$ales Gravy
P R E S S

Sales Gravy Press
The Sales Book Publisher™
P.O. Box 1389
Thomson, GA 30824

Published by Sales Gravy Press
Printed in the United States of America

Cover Design: Dave Blaker

First Edition

ISBN-13: 978-1-935602-09-5

Table of Contents

Introduction

In my long experience as a sales manager, I found that what I always needed most were ideas. In my years as a sales management consultant, I've found that my clients are always looking for ideas as well. The goal of *The Sales Management Guru's Guide to Sales Management* — and our other titles in the *Guru* series — is to give you ideas for developing a great sales organization — and, ultimately, boosting your company's revenues.

No question: Sales management is a tough job. You've got to build and lead a sales team. You've got to report to upper management. You're responsible to your peers and your customers — and, in many cases, to your company's vendors as well. This book is designed to help you address all those issues.

At Acumen Management, we know that sales leaders need ideas, concepts and tools to help them establish winning sales organizations — and we also know that they don't have much time. *The Sales Management Guru's Guide to Sales Management* is designed to provide you with a quick read that's packed with plenty of proven tools and real-world recommendations.

We've divided our advice into four key categories:

- Strategy & Planning
- Sales Management
- Hiring, Training & Compensation
- Culture

Within those categories, you'll learn about everything from goal-setting to time management to smart hiring to sales contests. Among other things, you'll learn how to measure your progress, develop cutting-edge training programs, create a competitive yet collaborative environment and, above all, build a top-notch, high-performance sales team.

Be sure to see the special report at the end, "The Job of Sales Management: A Prescriptive Approach to Defining Duties and Responsibilities." This bonus chapter describes a variety of specific actions that successful sales managers take to regularly exceed their goals.

Want more detail? See the Sales Management Guru's other guides:

- *The Sales Management Guru's Guide to Building Compensation Plans That Work!*
- *The Sales Management Guru's Guide to Recruiting High Performing Sales Teams.*
- *The Sales Management Guru's Ultimate Handbook for Sales Managers*

All are available on our Web site (www. AcumenManagement.com), where you can also purchase our DVDs that include five hours of training: *"Ignite Your*

Sales and Build Predictable Revenue - The Business of Strategic Sales Management" and Interactive *Sales-Management Tool Kit.*

Our Web site also includes many free white papers and videos and you'll find more free insights on our blog: www.YourSalesManagementGuru.com.

Meanwhile, please enjoy *The Sales Management Guru's Guide to Sales Management!*

Acknowledgements

After more than 25 years of working and consulting in sales management environments, I have so many individuals to acknowledge who have influenced my life and philosophies. Some have impacted my personal life, others my professional life and still others, both.

I'd like to start by acknowledging my mentors Sam Hagerman, a Boy Scout Camp Director in the early days of my life, as well as David Keene, President of Versyss, who offered me the opportunity to become a VP of Sales and gain the perspective of leading a major organization. There were countless individuals that I have worked with in my professional life that put up with me; each of you, I trust, knows your impact. Thank you.

In addition, I would like to thank my personal friends Dennis Pottebaum and Larry Decklever who continually offered positive reinforcement and support during my early days of becoming an entrepreneur. Also, Karen Winner, thank you for all your marketing ideas and insights in helping us position Acumen Management. I have truly enjoyed speaking and sharing our insights with thousands of individuals and working closely with many other independent consultants who have offered ideas and additional services to our clients. It has turned into a wonderful ride with so many benefits, mostly sharing my thoughts, ideas, tools, and systems with so many of our clients and seeing the positive impact on their organizations.

I need to thank Jeb Blount at Sales Gravy who came on board with the Sales Management Guru's focus on the toughest job in most organizations and is publishing our series of books.

Anne Stuart, my fabulous editor that had to work through all my ideas, broken sentences and created short, crisp ideas that will help sales organizations reach higher levels of achievement.

Lastly and most importantly, a huge thank you to my wife, Jolyne, who took the leap with me into this world of independence and uncertainty, while enduring many nights away from home and a seven day-a-week job focus. Her continuous faith and support has always been there for me.

I thank each of our clients for their support, encouragement and willingness to engage the Acumen philosophy of "building organizations through the execution of strategic sales management."

Ken Thoreson, President

Acumen Management Group Ltd.

www.YourSalesManagementGuru.com

PART I:
STRATEGY
&
PLANNING

1 | Planning Makes Perfect

Creating a successful plan that describes where you want your business to go is critical for assuring both profit and growth. Here are four steps to help you build your plan.

From the past 13 years of consulting with executives from companies of all sizes, focus areas and experience levels, I've found two common denominators among those that are growing and profitable: They all have clear visions for their companies (which we'll discuss in the next chapter) and they all have processes for developing business plans that allow them to execute effectively and measure their progress.

Many executives create budgets for their companies, but fail to create functional business, operating and sales/marketing plans as well. No matter what your company's focus, and regardless of whether you have a two- or 20+-person sales team, profitable growth requires developing a plan describing where you want your company to go. The idea is to spend more time working on the business, not just in the business.

A successful plan should include these four fundamental steps:

1. Define your business and personal goals.

Essentially, this means stating your vision for both your business and yourself. Frequently, goals focus solely on financial metrics, but you must also develop a set of personal or philo-

sophical beliefs to guide and improve your overall organizational performance. These beliefs may be based on the type
of team culture you want to foster, or they may be based on
employee- participation and client-satisfaction levels. These
business metrics and personal vision will become the basis
for your tactical sales plans.

The key issue at this step: focus on outcomes. Examples
include revenue growth, margin levels, partner recognition,
customer satisfaction levels, pre-tax margin percentages,
number of net new clients per quarter and account penetration goal.

2. Evaluate the business environment.

Identify the key business drivers that increase revenue and
reduce expenses. Consider market opportunity, the capabilities required to achieve your organization's goals and your
current and desired market positions.

The element of market opportunity is critical for setting
your sales objectives. For each product or service area in
which you focus, make the following calculations:

- Estimate the total number of potential buyers in the marketplace.
- Determine the total percentage of ideal buyers per year
  from that number.
- Estimate the average order size per transaction.
- Determine the percentage of sales opportunities you will
  participate in per year.
- Determine the win/loss percentage of your sales opportunities.

These figures will provide the data you need to build a

reasonably accurate sales plan and estimate your total costs to determine your ROI.

Before adding a new product or service offering, call potential customers in the market and ask them questions necessary to validate your assumptions.

3. Involve your business-management and sales teams.

Ask your management and sales teams to weigh in on questions such as:

- What went well — and not so well — in the past year?
- What are the key business assumptions for this year?
- What are the key metrics to be used to measure success in each department?
- What are the business opportunities for success?

This step's goal is to assess your chances for success, identify the key factors necessary to succeed and, most important, build your management and sales teams' commitment to achieving your business vision.

4. Validate your assumptions.

As you develop your plan, be realistic. Validate your assumptions by factoring in criteria such as the economic realities or vertical trends within your geographic area, competitors' positions within your market, your ability to differentiate your offerings and create unique value and the internal company resources that you need for success (people, capital and so on).

In developing your business plan, be sure to define, list and provide methods for measuring all ingredients in the proper sequence of preparation and execution. Each quarter, re-assess your execution and assumptions to ensure that you're still on track for profitability and growth. I recommend that you graphically track your trends and data. This visual representation will make it much easier for you and your management team to evaluate your progress.

2 | Value and Growth: Partners In Success

Leaders and managers need two key attributes — clear vision and specific objectives -- to develop the kind of business value that fuels company growth.

Building your business requires both leadership and management, and the first step in that journey is understanding the difference between the two.

Leadership is the ability to make things happen by encouraging and channeling others' contributions, addressing important issues and acting as a catalyst for change and continuous improvement. Management is the skill of attaining predefined objectives with others' cooperation and effort. Both are necessary for creating the business value that leads to growth.

In addition, the best organizations — of any size, in any industry -- are led by individuals who have two key attributes: clear vision and the ability to establish specific objectives for working toward their organizational goals. Executives at companies that have leveled off, stalled or are struggling just to break even may well lack both vision and objectives.

Creating Your Vision

An executive vision should address the following questions:

What does your organization look like now? What will it

look like in three years in terms of revenues, number of employees and specialty areas?

- How do you define success? What will the company's net worth be in three years? What are its profit goals?

- How do you want to be known by your clients, your competitors and the business community and your vendors??

- What's your ultimate goal? Do you have an exit strategy that calls for acquiring other companies or being acquired yourself? Or do you want to build a long-term corporate organization?

Considering these few key questions will help you fine-tune your vision, focus your efforts and inspire your employees. The answers will also help you (and your managers) set objectives to spur your company's growth.

Crafting Your Objectives

Among other considerations, sales-related objectives might include:

- Revenue growth objectives by dollars or percentage
- Gross margin dollars generated by product or service area
- Gross Margin Percentage and dollars by product or service area generated by new or current customers
- Revenue per employee
- Percentage of service dollars vs. products generated
- Managed services dollars vs. total revenue

- Number of net new clients added each quarter
- Percentage of won/lost accounts per proposal generation

Managers can use predefined objectives to create sales and marketing programs and dashboards to measure effectiveness. Leaders can use these objectives to judge management performance and promote the organization's continuous improvement. The probable results: Employee performance and morale will improve, customer satisfaction will increase, revenue and margin goals will be exceeded -- and your business will begin to build value.

Improving your organization's value is critical in both growing and maturing industries. Certainly, you can define value as retained earnings, recurring revenue values and balance sheet results, but it's also important to evaluate sales factors such as customer retention, net new client acquisition ratios or client penetration rates and lifetime value ratios.

Other important components to include in building long-term value: Your organization's intellectual property, patents, employee non-compete agreements, brand recognition and even employee retention percentages.

One last word: As a professional -- no matter what your specialty or your level of responsibility -- you must also focus on personal growth. What's your plan for increasing your individual value over the next year? Moving forward requires all of us to manage not only our companies' growth plans, but our own personal development as well.

3 | SCORECARD: HOW DO YOU RATE?

Use our balanced scorecard to evaluate your company's per-formance — and our pizza analogy to craft your approach for improvement.

Chances are that, around the beginning of every calendar year — or, perhaps, around the start of your fiscal year -- you assess how your organization is doing. You probably consider factors such as past successes, areas needing improvement and, most important, where you're headed.

Of course, it's helpful to have a tool to track your progress — one that you can use anytime. From working with hundreds of companies over the past 13 years, Acumen Management has developed a list of traits and values that characterize successful organizations. Grading your company against this list can provide a quick snapshot of how you're doing.

Before you begin, note that our scorecard isn't arranged to indicate priorities in terms of importance. However, for accurate results, you should ask: "How would my employees or other management team members score the organization on these topics?" Then consider their likely responses, as well as your own, in your answer. (Guru Hint: This quiz could be a great exercise for your next management meeting.)

To complete the scorecard, rate each item on a scale of 1-5, with 5 being the best. If you rate your company as a 5 in a particular area, it means that you believe that you've done everything possible to excel in that category. A rating of 3 indicates that you're making progress on addressing issues in this area. A 1 means that you know you're in trouble! Take a moment now to compile your ratings.

Scorecard	
Topic	Rating
Corporate culture is deep and consistent	
Business strategies come first	
Business development effectiveness is essential	
The best practices are consistent within my organization	
Sales is a corporate priority	
Structured process is key to success and we are focused in all departments	
Teamwork prevails in all departments	
Training and recruitment are critically important to our success	
Compensation is linked to corporate objectives	
Corporate image and branding is important	
Key to Scorecard Results	Total Score
Minor tuning may be needed	45-50
Improvement needed in specific areas	33-44
Multiple issues require prompt action	19-32
Problems organization-wide need immediate attention	0-18

Based upon your scores, the next questions you need to answer are: What are you going to do to achieve improvement where it's most needed -- and how and when are you going to do it?

We know that many companies need to address multiple scorecard issues, but aren't sure where to begin. If that's the case, you should start by focusing on a specific action plan for change.

I like to use a pizza analogy to illustrate the most effective approach. We all can easily describe our vision for the perfect pizza. We can see it and smell it; our mouths water at the mere thought of it. Your vision for your business should be at least that real. But, like a pizza, the list above is also divided into many "slices" --that is, topics that need to be addressed. And, as with a pizza, you're probably best off tackling just one slice at a time.

So if you rated your company low in several categories, pick just one "slice." Focus on fixing that segment for the next 30 to 60 days. Then choose another area to address for another month or so.

Meanwhile, keep this chapter handy so that in, say, six months, you can evaluate your progress. When you take the test again in a year, you'll be amazed at how far your company has come. Between now and then, visit our Web site and my blog for ideas to help you along the way: www.AcumenManagement.com and www.YourSalesManagementGuru.com.

4 | CREATING ORDER FROM CHAOS

Acumen's Situational Matrix of Sales Management helps you pinpoint exactly where your company stands in four critical areas, then create plans for improvement.

No matter what their size, truly effective companies use a systematic approach to managing all aspects of their operations—from incoming telephone calls the office to shipping products out to customers. They consider details and measure quality in all areas—including sales management.

In a business's early stages, the entrepreneur may do seat-of-the-pants selling along with every other aspect of the business. But as the company grows, effective, systematic and professional sales management becomes increasingly crucial. Understanding the sales management process—and documenting it and executing it effectively—will help differentiate the average companies from those that regularly exceed their revenue goals.

Rate Your Company

The more the company grows and changes, the more the person in charge of sales must put systems in place to create order from chaos. During my many years as a salesperson and sales manager, I've developed a theory that I call the Situational Matrix of Sales Management. In a nutshell, the theory states that the greater the company's potential to grow by offering new products or services, the more thoroughly it must define and manage its sales system.

This theory revolves around four components:

- The company's overall business position
- The maturity of company's products and services
- The effectiveness of its distribution channels
- The sophistication of the sales management systems.

To understand the concept, take a look at the diagram below. The left horizontal axis represents the company's overall business position; the right horizontal axis describes the effectiveness of its distribution channel. The upper vertical axis is defined by product or service maturity; the lower vertical axis represents the sophistication level of the sales-management systems.

Situational Matrix of Sales Management

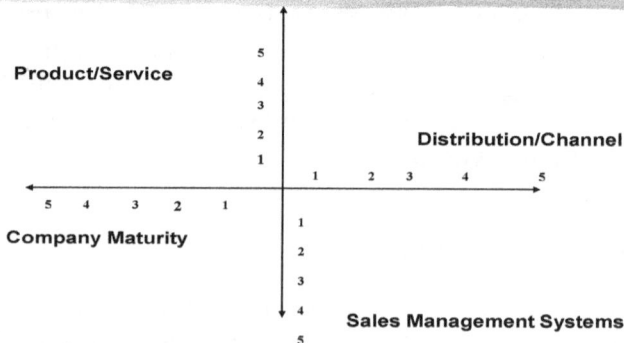

Product/Service

5
4
3
2
1

Distribution/Channel

1   2   3   4   5

5   4   3   2   1

Company Maturity

1
2
3
4
5

Sales Management Systems

Scale : 1= Early Stage-5= Highly Mature

Using a scale of 1 to 5, with 1 meaning "early stages" and 5 meaning "mature," rate each component 1 through 5 for your company.

Rate the company's overall business position (the left horizontal axis): 1 = Development Stage, 2 = Growth, 3 = Turnaround, 4 = Steady, 5 = Mature.

1. Rate the maturity of the direct or indirect distribution channel (the right horizontal axis): 1 = Nonexistent, 2 = Weak, 3 = Growth, 4 = Established, 5 = Dependable.

2. Rate the product/service position (the upper vertical axis): 1 = Creation stage, 2 = Launch, 3 = Market awareness, 4 = Market acceptance, 5 = Refinement.

3. Rate the sophistication level of sales-management systems (the lower vertical axis): 1 = None, 2 = Testing concepts, 3 = Minimal systems, 4 = Established process, 5 = Sophisticated reporting.

In the past, when markets and opportunities didn't move as quickly as they do in today's super-charged business climate, most companies' management processes moved along each axis at about the same speeds. So, for instance, if one component was working at a "4" level, then the others typically worked at similar levels.

That's no longer the case for rapidly growing companies that are launching new products and services. Today, things can quickly get out of balance, as demonstrated by situational matrix.

For instance, If a new product or service affects the company's maturity in terms of growth or turnaround, it requires a more sophisticated sales management process.

A development-stage or growth company entering new markets with new products must establish sales-management systems capable attracting, building and managing a distribution channel. Even in a mature company with an established distribution channel, a new Web-based e-commerce product will quickly changes all aspects of sales management, including recruitment, compensation, account management and measurement tools.

The company's overall situation affects all aspects of its sales-management process including strategies, sales goals, compensation and more. It provides a framework to begin developing or refining your current sales management plan. A solid plan enhances the sales leader's ability to clearly communicate vision, strategy and tactics and to set standards for sales-team performance.

To be successful and effective, sales management must undertake the necessary research, think through possible actions, develop focused processes and set standards of measurement. If an organization's revenues have flattened or declined, that often indicates that sales managers have failed or missed critical links in the sales management structure.

Components of a Sales Management Plan

The big question, of course, is how to start developing that structure.

A successful sales management plan must coordinate with the corporate business and marketing plans. People often ask how marketing and sales differ and how they work together. A common tongue-in-cheek answer is that marketing does the product positioning and planning, and if the plan doesn't work, the company fires the sales force and marketing creates a new plan. What this attitude reveals is that we measure sales by how well salespeople execute the company's overall business and marketing plans.

These areas should be defined in the company's sales management plan:

- Business and market overview

- Monthly activity tactical plan for a rolling six months, including trade shows, new product promotions, customer promotions, sales training

- Target account plan

- Sales organizational plan design for the next 24 months

- Definition of the sales process, measurement targets and channel strategy

- Sales technology plans and process

- Recruitment strategy, process and goals

- Development of strategic partners and alliances

- Revenue- and quota-forecasting tools and schedules

- Compensation plans and objectives

Elsewhere in this book, we examine various aspects of creating an effective sales management process in more detail—including how to keep the sales pipeline full while making time to accomplish the rest of the goals on your "to-do list."

5 | ADVISORY BOARDS: INSIGHTS THAT BOOST SALES

Advisory boards can improve relations with your clients while providing useful insights into how customers think and what they want.

Our research shows that accountability or, more accurately, the lack of accountability is among the top challenges that many companies face today. We've also found that many executives are too close to their own organizations to have genuine insight into their own businesses, their marketplaces or their industries. Client advisory boards and business advisory boards can help provide better visibility for both those blind spots.

Client Advisory Boards

A client advisory board, typically including five to seven current clients, can provide highly useful insights into customer needs from the customer perspective. For instance, the group might evaluate your sales and service functions or serve as a sounding board for new product ideas. Board members should be willing to meet formally with you at least three times a year and commit to at least two years of service. We recommend that you select not only your "pet" clients, but a cross-section of your customers.

At first, someone from your company should set agendas, oversee advisory-board meetings and take detailed notes. Eventually, you may want to encourage a client-company board member to take over managing the sessions Regardless of who's running the sessions, it's critical for you and your own management team to avoid becoming defensive regarding issues that board members raise during their meetings.

However, it's equally important to remind all attendees that these sessions shouldn't be viewed as complaint forums, but instead as opportunities to work together toward improved performance. If a meeting drifts toward becoming a gripe session, whoever is running the session should immediately redirect the discussion.

What's the sales angle? The simple fact that you have an advisory board can be an important asset during the sales process. Chances are that prospects in your market area will recognize your board members, and they're also likely to be impressed with your commitment to the customer experience.

Within a vertical market, you might also create an industry advisory board with members such as past trade-association presidents, respected industry consultants and current clients. This committee can provide market insights and ideas for future offerings, and, like a client advisory board, it can serve as a sales differentiator.

Generally, members of such boards aren't compensated, but you might acknowledge their contributions with small gifts or special product or service offers.

Business Advisory Boards

A business advisory board's role is to recommend strategy,

suggest solutions to business problems and advise on relevant regulations. Like a client advisory board, it should include five to seven members, but all should be from outside your company. The best such panel will have a diverse mix of local businesspeople and specialists from key functional areas such as human resources, finance, marketing and sales.

This type of committee typically meets quarterly, but can convene more frequently if needed. We recommend that meetings follow formal agendas that are sent to attendees in advance, along with any supporting information that's needed for discussion. Such preparation is essential, otherwise it may appear that your company doesn't take the advisory group seriously or is unwilling to share important information with its members. and those members may stop participating as a result.

The two main benefits that you can expect from a business advisory board are insight and accountability. For many executives (their current businesses are the only ones they've managed and led) outside expertise can be particularly valuable.

Some Acumen clients work with their business advisory boards to conduct regular operational reviews. This process not only helps hold the management team accountable for results, but creates a situation in which the entire company is accountable to the business advisory board.

Keep in mind that members of business advisory boards are normally reimbursed for their time; occasional gifts of appreciation are also appropriate.

One other option: join or form a peer group. A peer group consists of business owners in a particular industry, typically from noncompeting companies in the same geographic area. By providing an environment where you can share your knowledge and concerns with like-minded professionals, a peer group lets you create another form of partnership — one based on a sense of community.

6 | TAKING A VERTICAL VIEW

What does it take to sell in a niche market? Consider this advice before you dive in.

The first thing most people ask when considering whether to focus on vertical or niche markets is, of course, what are the benefits? Plenty, in Acumen's experience. They include:

- Higher revenues
- Better margins
- Lower cost of sales
- Increased velocity of order flow
- Bigger average order size

If those advantages are enough to convince you that it's time to "think narrow," it's time to select your target verticals. Your ultimate objective is shifting your company's philosophy from being a vendor to a being a member of the industry you want to sell into. Create a positioning statement determining what that industry offers you and what you can bring to it. Then take the following nine steps to learn about, and begin moving into, those markets.

Going Vertical, Step by Step

1. **Create a market profile.** List the top five characteristics for the ideal client in each vertical industry or niche market. Undertake basic market research to identify the gross number of clients in the market. Even more important: Determine the number of clients that match the ideal characteristics that you've established.

2. **Identify initial sales targets.** Using the market profile, pinpoint the top 150 prospects in each vertical. For example, you might identify all companies with annual revenues of $10 million or more, or that have at least 100 employees, or that have three or more locations, or that serve at least five states (or any other criteria that you consider important). Begin building a database with information on these prospects.

3. **Identify key industry groups.** Locate the top local and national industry associations for each vertical. Develop lists of key industry trade shows, relevant monthly meetings and the names of current and past association leaders. Plan to attend every trade show and at least half the monthly gatherings. Increase your visibility by becoming active on an association committee.

4. **Identify key industry publications/sites.** Industry magazines, Web sites and newsletters can keep you abreast of major issues facing your vertical-market clients and prospects. Subscribe to and read these vehicles. If possible, try to write for them as well. Obtain their editorial calendars (often available online) and offer to contribute articles or columns that fit in with their coverage and showcase your expertise.

5. **Identify key industry influencers.** Find the top consultants, lawyers, accountants and others who service and market to your target industries. Work with them to

share contacts and create joint referral networks. Touch base with these sources at least quarterly. Not sure which groups, publications and influencers carry the most weight in a specific market? Ask your clients and prospects — and follow up on their advice.

6. **Identify potentially useful partners**. Make contact with at least five companies that sell related, but non-competing, goods or services to your chosen vertical markets. You can find these types of businesses at trade shows and through ads in industry publications. You may wish to explore developing joint marketing programs, or you may just consider working out lead-sharing agreements. We call these companies "business ecosystem partners." Developing relationships with them will broaden your expertise and your acceptance in the market.

7. **Identify key contacts.** Develop a detailed database for each vertical-industry prospect, customer and influencer organization. Include at least five names and titles for each organization, pinpointing a main contact at each company.

8. **Develop training and certification programs.** Succeeding in a vertical market requires that your team stay current on all that industry's issues. Develop ongoing programs to train employees in industry-specific sales skills and, if necessary, certify their knowledge of particular technologies, products or services. Assign sales team members to attend workshops at conferences, this will assist your team to better understand the issues facing their prospects.

9. **Measure, modify, monitor.** Moving into any vertical market will probably involve facing established competitors. That means it's especially critical to track the effectiveness of all sales plans, marketing materials, initiatives and events, modifying them as necessary. As always, it's

also important to monitor customer satisfaction as thoroughly as possible.

Ultimately, the secret of succeeding in any vertical market is knowing as much as you can about the industry: its issues, its companies and, most of all, its people.

7 | THE HALFWAY POINT

Somewhere around the six-month mark, it's smart to assess whether you're still on target to meet your goals for the current year.

Are you on track? By midyear, you should know the answer to that question—that is, whether you're still headed in the right direction to meet your year-end goals.

Here are a few other questions that you should be able to answer at the halfway point:

- Are you consistently achieving your revenue/margin goals every month?
- Are you consistently achieving your sales quotas every month?
- Have you increased your number of net new clients?

If you're on track to achieve your goals for the current year, great! If you're coming up short, it's time to stop and reassess before you look to the last quarter and begin planning for next year. Time moves fast and the actions required to fix your situation won't happen overnight.

When we conduct strategic business planning with

clients, we often create tracking metrics for month-to-month evaluation and graphical trend analysis for quarterly use. (For more on this topic, see a related article, "Planning Makes Perfect.") By measuring your progress against specific objectives, you can begin to gauge your organization's ability to execute for the rest of the year.

But before you start measuring, step back and consider these three issues:

- Were your original objectives realistic?
- Did you create action plans or programs designed to achieve those objectives?
- If so, how effectively did you execute against those plans?

Let's look at each issue in more depth.

Reality Check

In working with most organizations, we often find that unrealistic objectives prevented them from hitting their targets. Typically, the objectives were unrealistic because management didn't anticipate adverse "environmental" factors. Such factors might include unfavorable market conditions, product offerings that missed market timing or failed to meet market expectations, or internal issues such as having an unqualified sales team, not hiring aggressively to attain revenue goals or insufficiently trained technical staff.

Here's an example based on that last factor. With the release of a new version of a popular product, you might anticipate that a certain percentage of your client base would want to upgrade. But if you didn't have enough employees trained to implement or sell the new product/service, or did not create/execute a well throughout marketing plan you'd have missed the market opportunity. In that case, an internal issue is preventing you from reaching an important goal. Keeping such issues in mind is important for developing realistic objectives.

Taking Action

In other cases, entrepreneurs have their visions and goals clearly in mind and understand their environments as well. But they, too, sometimes miss the mark, often because they haven't developed specific action plans.

The best businesspeople know how to convert their visions and goals into written, tactical, executable programs. They also ensure that all their employees understand the objectives and their own roles in achieving those goals. In our strategic planning process, we call this "building commitment," and it's also a critical component for hitting your annual targets.

Effective Execution

In still other situations, companies have realistic goals and excellent plans for achieving them -- but fall short anyway. While environmental reasons could be to blame, we often find that the real problem is management's failure to execute on those excellent marketing and sales plans and other initiatives.

Here's the solution: During strategic planning, these companies should define key milestone dates to review how effectively they're executing their plans and, if necessary, to set new objectives for fine-tuning their course toward their targets. The plan should also build in accountability at every level of the organization, with each phase including solid metrics and time frames that define success.

Carefully considering these questions will not only help ensure that you're on target for your year-end goals, but greatly increase your chances of hitting a bull's-eye.

8 | SPRINT TO THE FINISH

Your own sense of urgency may be driven by upcoming deadlines for quotas or bonuses, but you need to show prospects how moving forward now meets their needs rather than yours.

At this writing, the economy seems to be coming back from the worst recession in decades. But even in good times, ending the year on a high note is more challenging than it used to be.

We've been offering the following advice to our clients and their sales teams as they prepare for the end of the year.

- **Keep things in perspective.** No matter what's happening with the economy, people and businesses need products and services. Focus on what's most in demand these days: solutions that can increase efficiency, cut costs and enhance customer relationships.

- **Stay optimistic.** In good times and bad, remember that clients and prospects are seeking help. Again, you're in a position to both reassure and assist them.

- **Work harder.** (Sorry, but that's what's needed). Try to stay out in front by stretching yourself both in terms of attracting new customers and better serving existing ones. Sell professionally; execute brilliantly.

Finishing in Top Form

Meanwhile, the standard end-of-year scenario still applies. As always, this is when accelerated compensation programs kick in. More important, it's when many management bonus systems take effect, rewarding executives for driving certain levels of pretax income to the bottom line or attaining their revenue targets. Throw in the need to fill sales pipelines for early next year, and it's no wonder that, just like every year at this time, sales teams feel like they're in the last 100 yards of a big race.

Following are five additional steps to help you stay out in front as you approach this year's finish line:

1. **Count the days.** In the same way that consumers track holiday shopping days, know how long you've got left to sell this year. Doing the countdown adds urgency to the process for you and your prospects. Try to answer this question: How can you use the remaining weekends to boost business?

2. **Consider all your resources.** Can you turn to colleagues to strategize about opportunities and develop winning tactics? Consider customer on-site reference visits? Can an existing client or vendor help create credibility with prospects?

3. **Plot closing strategies.** Think about why prospects need your solution and exactly how they'll benefit from implementing it, whether it's generating revenues, improving productivity or better serving customers. Then figure out a reason for them to act now. You may be focused

on earning those year-end bonuses or making those all-important quotas, but you need to show prospects how moving forward at this point will benefit them, not just you. (Guru Hint: Schedule formal prospect pipeline sales strategies with other salespeople twice each week.)

4. **Make contact twice weekly.** Never let a week slip by between meetings with prospects. If you see them on Tuesdays, see them again on Thursdays. Stop by at a convenient time--but always have a valuable reason to visit, such as providing implementation plans or a reference letters.

5. **Keep prospecting.** Sales organizations often drain their pipelines by the end of December. January may be strong with leftover business, but February, March and April typically lag. It's important to ensure that marketing and prospecting levels remain constantly focused on future pipeline development. We recommend that you take your calendar and block out specific times for prospecting between now and the end of the year.

One last tip for coping with a recovering economy: In the downturn following the 9/11 terrorist attacks, I developed a short personal motto that successfully reinforced the need to keep moving forward. It was: "Take action. Stay positive."

I suggest that you develop a similar slogan to help you navigate these still-uncertain times. Having a strong foundation can make all the difference in how you finish out the current year and position yourself for the next one.

9 | SCORECARD: GAUGING PROCESS, SETTING GOALS

Use this handy scorecard to evaluate your organization's effectiveness and develop priorities for improvement in the coming year.

Every December, I write down my personal and business goals for the coming year. I also review my goals from the previous year and grade my performance in meeting them. I've saved these sheets for the past two decades and I find that reviewing them is a telling experience.

In another chapter, entitled "How Do You Rate," I challenged sales managers to take a similar approach to evaluating their companies and targeting overall areas for improvement. If you took the initial quiz, spend a few minutes repeating the exercise to gauge your progress. If you didn't, consider taking it now to get a big-picture view of where your organization stands today. Either way, you'll quickly see where you're doing well and where you still need work. (As an aside, you may wish to take the free sales management assessment on our website, www.AcumenManagement.com).

Meanwhile, evaluating your current status in 10 specific sales-management areas is a great way to leap into the New Year.

Using the "report card" on the next page, grade your

organization on a scale of 1 to 5, with 5 being the highest.
As in the earlier evaluation:

- A '5' rating indicates that you feel you've done everything possible to excel in that area.
- A '3' rating indicates that you're making progress in that category.
- A '1' rating means that you know you're in trouble!

Take a moment now to compile your ratings:

Year-End Sales Management Report Card	
Question	**Rating** **(1=low; 5=high)**
At the start of each month, how confident are you about having enough potential business in your pipeline's current stage to exceed the current sales budget?	
How confident are you that your pipeline has enough potential business in the 30-, 60- and 90-day categories to exceed future monthly quotas?	
How well are all key accounts targeted? How effective are your plans for attacking them?	
How effective is your hiring process in terms of selecting the best candidates, not just the best available candidates?	
How good are your initial sales-training programs and your plans for ongoing salesperson development?	
How good is your CRM/SFA system in terms of being up to date, used effectively and backed up regularly?	

How well does your compensation plan work? How well are company goals aligned with compensation and quota programs?	
Key to Scorecard Results	**Total Score**
Minor tuning may be needed	41-50
Improvement needed in specific areas	31-40
Multiple issues require prompt action	21-30
Problems organization-wide need immediate attention	0-20

Interpreting Your Score

The results of your evaluation not only indicate how your sales organization is doing overall, but also identify specific areas you can target for improvement in the coming year. These areas are all critical for building high-performance sales teams and increasing revenue predictability — issues that ultimately affect your entire company.

For that reason, sales executives and business owners alike should know a few basic ratios, metrics or numbers, such as the ratio of potential revenues in the pipeline to both the defined quotas and the sales actually attained each month.

From tracking this information over six to nine months, you'll determine your forecasting accuracy ratios — that is, the dollar value of your forecasts as compared with the actual sales achieved — and the value of the sales opportunities that you need at the start of each month to attain your sales quotas. Other critical numbers to know include your win/loss ratio (number of proposals versus the number of wins) and the accuracy of each salesperson's monthly forecasts.

One other Guru Hint: Make a resolution to avoid the "out of sight, out of mind" problem in the coming year. Each month, for each major sales opportunity in your pipeline, create a written plan of tactics for closing the account. Keep those action plans prominently on display on your desk or whiteboard. Doing so will help ensure that you're aware of your important prospects. Increasing the focus on closing a few extra major sales opportunities each year will ensure you exceed your sales objectives.

10 | LOOKING BACK, LOOKING AHEAD

Recent years have been especially rough on sales teams, but even the most difficult times provide valuable insights that you can carry forward.

When your sales organization turns the calendar page to a fresh new year, it's tempting to simply forget about the past one — especially if it was challenging. But analyzing the previous year's performance is among the best ways to improve the current year's results.

Here are eight questions to consider, along with our recommendations for building on what you've learned.

1. **What can you learn from reviewing your entire calendar from last year?**

   Look for patterns and empty spaces. Did you have enough scheduled appointments? Were the appointments you scheduled worthwhile? Did you make the best use of your time? Did you find any account names you had forgotten about — ones that you should follow up on this year? As a result of reviewing last year's calendar, what changes in scheduling will you make in this year?

2. **What can you learn from honestly reviewing each sales opportunity you lost last year?**

    Were you creative, or did you simply work as if you were on autopilot? Were you ever really in the running for the opportunities you lost—or were you simply comparison fodder? What could you have done differently, if anything, to have won those opportunities? By the way, this is a good topic for a sales-team meeting. Ask each person to discuss two lost opportunities, then have the entire team perform a loss analysis. (Guru Hint: You can also use the same exercise to let team members share how and why they each won two opportunities.)

3. **Did you grow professionally last year?**

    Did you increase your sales, organizational, technical or industry-related skills during the past 12 months? How many books or seminars did you read or attend? What steps will you take to improve your level of professionalism in each quarter of this year?

4. **Last year, how many new people did you meet who can help you network? What will you do to increase your networking capability this year?**

    Actively building business relationships is critical for your team's ongoing success. This year, each salesperson should establish at least five relationships with non-competitive contacts that sell into the same types of accounts. That kind of networking can offer valuable benefits: those contacts may refer salespeople into accounts they didn't know about before—or provide them with information that can help them win when new opportunities open up.

5. **Did you expand your social media and sales technology exposure last year?**

   How actively did you use LinkedIn, Facebook, Jigsaw, Microsoft CRM and other tools to expand your sales reach? Did you use LinkedIn to develop your relationships or identify and reach out to new prospects? How many LinkedIn knowledge groups did you join last year? More important, did you contribute value to the groups you joined? What other groups might you join and contribute to this year?

6. **How well did you take care of yourself last year?**

   Especially in challenging times, everyone needs time to recharge. What did you do to keep yourself in shape physically last year? Did you take up or expand on a hobby? This year, try to make a point of relaxing and having some fun. That will help you stay fresh. Finding professional balance and personal balance is one of the biggest secrets to success.

7. **What was your hourly earnings rate last year?**

   Most important, how many selling hours -- time spent face-to-face with prospects -- did you log last year? In reality, due to holidays, weekends, vacations, sick days and so forth, you really only have about 10.5 months in a year to make a 12-month quota. Did you track your time last year? What do you want your hourly earnings rate to be this year? Try this: Take your desired annual income. Divide that figure by the number of real selling hours in the year (and be honest about those actual selling hours). The resulting figure should represent your hourly billing rate. How will you achieve that rate this year? How will you become more efficient? Be greedy with your time.

8. **Did your sales formula work last year?**

   Take time to determine last year's basic numbers. How many face-to-face meetings did you make with a pre-sales technical rep? How many demonstrations, proposals or executive presentations did you make? Calculate these numbers by each month and then compare your results. Did you exceed your quota last year? If not, what will you do this year to ensure that you do so this year? What activities need to be increased to achieve your sales budgets?

You've heard the famous definition of insanity: doing the same thing over and over again and expecting different results. Here's my corollary: Focus on new ideas and actions and expect better results. Let's all focus on making the current year a successful and prosperous one.

PART II:

SALES

MANAGEMENT

11 | FIXING A BROKEN SALES ORGANIZATION

The company you're about to "visit" is fictional, but its trib-ulations may sound all too familiar. Keep reading for real-life advice on making repairs and boosting morale.

Over the past 12 years, I've worked with executives, managers and employees at companies of all types and sizes throughout North America and in other countries as well. While every client engagement has been unique, I've identified some common cultural problems that can prevent companies from reaching their full business potential. Among the most widespread issues: weak, disorganized or dysfunctional strategic sale management.

To illustrate what can go wrong, let's take a guided tour through a hypothetical client company that embodies many of the problems I've encountered over the years. We'll use "Law & Order" rules here: "Although inspired in part by true incidents, the following story is fictional and does not depict any actual person or event."

First Impressions

Walking into the front office, we see a few chairs and a few outdated vendor awards on the walls. Employees walk by a visitor without offering a greeting or showing any enthusiasm. Empty waiting areas and expressionless employees don't tend to create a positive first impression for prospects visiting the office.

Let's continue our tour by meeting the cast.

The President

First, I meet with "Bill," the company president. In Bill's office, we chat about his business, his vision, his frustrations and his business's the lack of profitability. My experienced ears hear Bill saying about his salespeople: "They don't get it;" "They don't work hard enough;" "They really don't know how to sell the company's products or services;" "They don't seem to care about the business as much as he does."

Bill also thinks that his sales manager focuses too much on non-sales issues. When I ask Bill whether he's discussed those concerns with the sales manager, he says he's been too busy. When I ask whether he meets monthly with the manager to agree on priorities, Bill says the person should already understand those priorities.

A Vice President

Bill introduces me to his vice president of professional services. During the first 10 minutes of our 45-minute discussion, I hear a lot about how the engineers spend time helping salespeople in every engagement, only to see the sales teams get all the credit. "They never take the time to really learn about the products," the VP says of the salespeople. "If it weren't for my team and their expertise, we would have no sales." When I ask the VP when he last held a training session to teach salespeople what they should know, I get a shrug.

The Salespeople

As I interview the company's salespeople, either face to face or on the phone, I begin to connect the dots between their comments and the complaints I heard from the president and vice president.

The salespeople say things like: "Management always seems to dominate every opportunity." "Management is always micro-managing what I do." "Sales meetings are brutal; everything seems so disorganized." "Creating proposals is a joke; it takes forever for everyone to approve or rewrite every sentence." "Management seems to change what we do every 90 days." "Management never seems to know what's going on."

Something else emerges from my recorded interviews with each salesperson: When asked, "Why do people buy from you," each one has a different answer. Confusion is everywhere.

Assessing Your Own Company

While these particular scenarios are fictional, the conversations they represent are, sadly, all too real among many clients we have served.

Does anything here ring a bell about how your people think about the company, their jobs—and each other? If so, this is an excellent time to assess whether you need to fix your company's management processes, and, by extension, the organization's morale. Here are a few steps toward making repairs in both areas:

- Create an ongoing sales-training program that involves other departments; product/services, company operations, product knowledge, sales skills.

- Run monthly company meetings to bring all employee teams together. Those sessions create a great environment for discussing the company's philosophy and objectives.

- Improve communications. For example, send out e-mails announcing success stories. Hold breakfast meetings with groups of employees to gather their feedback on their own departments or on cross-departmental issues.

- Recognize achievement with awards and rewards.

- Encourage management to create task forces focused on achieving corporate objectives.

- Make "soft" cultural improvements to increase morale and teamwork. For instance, set up meetings or teams to brainstorm ideas for new products and services. Establish reward programs to recognize people for successful cost-saving ideas or improvements in customer-service programs.

Creating a positive atmosphere and keeping your entire organization in good working order requires ongoing requires time, vision, energy and commitment to continuous improvement—which, by the way, is the definition of leadership.

12 | TIME MANAGEMENT FOR SALES LEADERS

Try these tactics for making the best possible use of one of your most valuable resources.

Recently, I posted a question in several of my LinkedIn forums asking, "What are the top three challenges for sales managers?"

The No. 1 response, by a wide margin: time management.

Sales management is a high-churn profession. Many managers only last about 18 months in the job due to the challenges of dealing with employee issues, achieving quotas, meeting middle- and executive-management demands and managing the business. In addition, many sales managers have never received proper training or been exposed to successful role models.

We've found that the sales-management role is a weak link in many companies. We find that as we address sales leaders' time-management problems, we begin to resolve other company issues as well.

A Time for Everything

We offer the following time-management tips for sales managers:

1. **Plan effectively and plan for chaos.** Sales meetings and sales-training sessions must be defined with agendas and organized 90 days in advance. A little planning enables well-run meetings with relevant content and decreases the likelihood of people missing training sessions because "something else came up." But don't overplan your daily schedule. Leave time to respond to unanticipated problems and situations. (Guru Hint: Schedule important one-on-one meetings for 7:30 a.m. — before you get distracted with other demands.)

2. **Don't accept every problem.** Often, a new or inexperienced sales manager tries to resolve every issue that sales or marketing employees bring up. That's understandable. Troubleshooting makes managers feel important, and it's human nature to want to be liked and respected for getting things done.

   The result of taking on every problem is that arises that the sales manager's "to-do" list gets longer and longer while the time available to accomplish the action items gets shorter and shorter. This situation can also generate emotional conflict between salespeople and the sales manager, with employees feeling that the manager can't get anything done and the manager feeling frustrated and emotionally drained by all the demands.

   Instead, when salespeople approach you with problems, ask them to recommend solutions — and, if possible, to handle implementing those solutions for you. I like to ask: "What are three solutions that could resolve the issue? And one that doesn't cost anything?" Training your employees to think through both problems and potential solutions allows them to begin to solve challenges on their own before coming to you!

3. **Seek good examples.** Managers often struggle if they haven't had first-hand experience with mentors or successful role models as sales managers. We recommend visiting or benchmarking similar companies to view how they run their sales organizations.

   Or you could form a peer group. When I was a vice president of sales at one company, I started a national sales-management association. Twice a year, I brought my colleagues together to share their experiences and collaborate on resolving common sales-management challenges. The result: Instead of just reacting to issues or events, many sales managers became more proactive, solving problems and even heading off potential headaches *before* they arose.

4. **Don't re-invent the wheel.** Many managers spend too much time creating new tools, sales programs or operational process documents. Use existing tools or ask your colleagues to share theirs with you. (See *Acumen's Interactive "Sales Manager's Tool Kit,"* which includes many tools that we've created for our clients, at www.AcumenManagement.com.)

5. **Keep your "to-do" list up to date.** Update or reprioritize your daily to-do lists-every evening. Make it a goal to do those updates before leaving the office—that way, you start the following day fresh, with a plan. My own system is to mark with an "A" the top items that I need to address and complete on a particular day.

6. **Set weekly goals.** While getting things accomplished every day is critical, be sure to prioritize weekly goals as well. Make sure those goals are clear and specific and at-

tainable. The best sales managers are focused. They know what they need to do, and they understand the difference between motion and direction. You can be very busy and in motion while not actually accomplishing what's needed: moving forward.

We all have the same amount of time each week to achieve our objectives — some of us just do so more effectively than others. I recently met a salesperson who made 11 to 13 face-to-face calls a week and spent one hour a day prospecting. Think he was organized? One of my mentors worked four days a week and enjoyed Fridays on Cape Cod -- and he was a partner in and vice president of sales for a large company with multiple offices.

If you focus on spending time like the valuable asset that it is, you'll accomplish more than anyone else in your office and outperform your competitors, too.

13 | MAKE MONDAY-MORNING MEETINGS COUNT

Use a well-organized, performance-oriented gathering to motivate your team for the coming week.

When we at Acumen undertake consulting engagements, we always sit in on clients' Monday-morning sales meetings.

That's because we know from experience that a weekly kick-off meeting is among the best ways to build a high-performance sales organization. A well-run Monday meeting puts everyone on the right track for the week ahead and helps the sales manager establish the discipline, control and accountability that every team needs.

Plan Ahead

Sales meetings may occur on the phone, if you have a remote sales team or in face-to-face sessions. But no matter what format they're in, these critical weekly meetings will be more successful if everyone involved knows what to expect.

First, all salespeople should be prepared to share their actions and results from the past week and their plans for the coming one, including what appointments they've made.

Next, you should work from an agenda, using the same

format every week. This step helps everyone know what's being covered and, of course, helps keep meetings on track and on time.

Finally, meetings should begin no later than 8:30 a.m. and last no more than an hour.

A Seven-Section Schedule

The following is a standardized sales-meeting agenda, divided into seven main sections.

- **Section 1:** Ask each salesperson to rate the previous week's performance on a scale of 1 to 5, with 5 being "great." This step increases accountability and gets everyone talking early in the meeting. Next, assign someone to take notes documenting any sales discussions and action items. Instruct your scribe to e-mail those notes to the whole team within 24 hours of the meeting. (Guru Hint: As the sales leader, you should review and approve the notes before they're circulated.)

- **Section 2:** Move to the sales pipeline and forecast discussions. Engage salespeople in strategy discussions that focus on their individual monthly sales commitments and forecasts. In addition, ask them to recommend potential tactical sales actions that other salespeople might take. This portion of the agenda will probably take the most time, and it's important to keep everyone's attention during the sales-strategy discussion. (Guru Hint: As you review each individual salesperson's forecast, ask other team members to share additional sales ideas. This will keep everyone engaged and encourage all members to help each other in selling.)

- **Section 3:** Review your month-to-date and year-to-date

goals against actual performance. Typically, these maybe sales versus quotas; these numbers may reflect sales goals by product/services or goals by salesperson. In addition, the sales manager should review all scorecards or other metrics that you're tracking.

- **Section 4:** Discuss all marketing events planned for the next 60 days. This step gives the whole team a heads-up about what's coming and an idea about what everyone needs to do to ensure event success. You marketing team should attend at least one sales meeting a month.

- **Section 5:** Review all sales-training meetings and topics planned for the next 90 days. Summarize not just the dates and times, but what sales skills will be discussed and what product, industry and organizational knowledge will be covered. You may wish to have individual salespeople handle some aspects of training sessions.

- **Section 6:** Consider this the catch-all part of the meeting. Summarize any administrative or technical issues, sales-contest information and other company topics that you may need to address.

- **Section 7:** Close the meeting on an "up" note. You might ask each salesperson for one "PMT" — a positive mental thought — that can be personal or professional in nature. This step builds camaraderie and sets the right tone for the coming week.

Building a high-performance sales team takes work, energy and organization. Starting the week with a high-quality sales meeting helps everyone begin the week focused, organized and ready to execute as effectively as possible.

14 | SALES & MARKETING: FRIENDS, NOT FOES

When these two key departments work together, both sides benefit. When they don't, you may be leaving money on the table. Focus on these four areas to create strong relationships.

Sales and marketing departments, which must work together in a symbiotic, supportive way, too often get bogged down in turf wars.

In fact, as much as 88 percent of marketing expenditures on lead generation and sales collateral are wasted because the sales team ignores these efforts, according to research from Aberdeen Group, a Boston-based IT research firm. Many sales teams apparently don't trust the materials they receive from marketing departments and opt instead to prepare their own. Such teams, typically, spend 40 to 60 hours a month re-creating customer-relevant collateral material, according to Aberdeen's research.

In working with one IT company, we at Acumen found that the organization's marketing staff generated an average of 72 leads a month, but few of those leads ever showed up in the sales pipeline analysis. Ultimately, that situation created serious finger-pointing: Marketing blamed sales for not following up effectively. Sales claimed that marketing's leads didn't pan out.

Many such problems stem in part from the two departments failing to understand each other's roles. Another issue is internal political posturing. Sales teams often feel that because they're the ones on the firing line, they should receive all the credit for bringing in revenue. Marketers, on the other hand, often feel ignored or unappreciated; they'd like acknowledgement for their role in sales.

This cultural clash impedes revenue generation at a time when marketing is increasingly called upon to support sales and track ROI.

Recommended Roles

We feel that marketing's role today should be to position the company uniquely in the marketplace, ensuring that events and other business-building activities are effectively coordinated and properly run to create the sales opportunities.

Meanwhile, salespeople should focus on properly executing the company's positioning, rather than putting their own "spin" on what management has determined is the company's value proposition.

We recommend that companies serious about improving the effectiveness of their sales-marketing relationships by focusing on these four key areas.

1. **Communication.** Marketing should participate in at least one monthly sales meeting. Agenda items should include communication between sales and marketing, messaging, lead results, market feedback and competition, as well as upcoming events and company programs.

2. **Metrics.** Remember, you can't manage what you don't measure. It's always wise, of course, to track win/loss rates, lead quantity and quality, lead source and lead

source/win ratio--you need to know where your leads are coming from and what source is achieving your best win result. While many organizations only track sales numbers, we recommend measuring marketing's contributions as well. Doing so will ensure that both teams are working toward the same goals. It also helps both sides determine what's working and what's not.

3. **Collaboration.** We recommend that marketing personnel not only work trade shows with salespeople, but also regularly observe sales calls, demonstrations and executive presentations. Taking those steps can help marketers create far more effective programs and materials.

4. **Compensation.** Consider creating mutual compensation plans that also rewards marketing when sales achieves its quarterly objectives. In some cases, we've recommended giving marketing a quarter-end bonus and an increase in its next quarter's budget when sales makes its numbers.

Finally, from an organizational perspective, sales and marketing should report to one executive to ensure that they're focused on the same corporate strategy. That may sound obvious, but when we examine why organizations fail, we often see that their marketing and sales departments have dramatically different perspectives about issues as basic as the company's greater goals. Making sure that both parties are playing for the same team will go a long toward ensuring everyone's success.

15 | PICKING THE RIGHT PARTNERS

Strategic sales partnerships can provide significant benefits for both parties — and for your customers as well.

$\mathbf{A}$t Acumen, we've found that today's most successful businesses tend to excel in six critical areas of sales management:

1. Understanding their clients' business needs
2. Maintaining selectivity and effective account segmentation and penetration
3. Developing solid strategies for handling their key accounts
4. Improving how salespeople manage their time, their accounts and their territories
5. Using all available resources as effectively as possible
6. Constantly strengthening their efforts to win market share

If your company isn't hitting home runs in all those areas, you may want to consider partnering with other organizations to help improve your performance.

Working with partners can provide you with the

additional knowledge that you may need to better understand a particular client's needs or more readily identify prospective accounts. Your partners may be able to introduce you to important contacts, purchasing patterns and corporate strategies. Their sales and technical teams may be able to help yours make joint presentations and proposals, better serve mutual territories and accounts or create true business solutions for customers.

In the long run, joining forces can help both parties improve their market positioning and achieve higher sales goals.

Building Beneficial Relationships

You can choose among several types of partnerships. While space limitations prevent us from exploring them in depth here, some of your options are:

- Business partnerships, which are designed to increase asset bases, expand the numbers and types of products or services offered and improve competitive advantage for both parties (possibly involving a formal merger or acquisition).

- Business-ecosystem partnerships, which involve organizations that sell related but non-competitive products and services into commonly shared markets.

- Market-alliance partnerships, which allow two companies to share leads, establish salesperson-to-salesperson relationships and pay each other for referrals.

- Strategic-alliance partnerships, which involve working with vendors that can provide your business with leads and support.

- Alliance/consulting relationships, in which companies exchange mutually beneficial services, such as serving on each other's advisory boards.

Business-ecosystem partnerships are where many organizations can gain the greatest leverage. They may be geographically based or within similar vertical markets. In any case, the power of leverage allows both sales organizations to be trained — at least in part — on each other's offerings. They can also develop common marketing programs. Ideally, your organization could expand to four to five business ecosystem partners. Ultimately, you'll gain access to mutual customer databases and create more complete added-value solutions.

Partnering Questions and Answers

Before opening talks with any potential partners, it's smart to seek answers to a few important questions:

- **Numbers:** How many users does the other company have in your market? Knowing this number will help you gauge how well the other party knows your customer base.

- **Expertise:** What domain knowledge does the other party offer that your team lacks? What additional value or expertise or benefits does that company bring to your solutions?

- **Alignment:** How well do you understand your potential partner's culture and value proposition? Are they in alignment with yours?

- **Reasons:** Why does this company want to partner with you? What can you offer the other party?

Finally, remember that partnerships take time to develop. Successful ones involve:

- **Trust,** which evolves from commitment, communication, strong performance and, most important, both parties consistently following through on their promises.

- **Innovation**, which stems from the new opportunities that the relationship opens up for each organization.

- **A set of metrics**, which involves having solid, mutually acceptable methods for measuring how well each company is meeting the other's expectations and how both organizations are progressing toward their goals.

The metrics should be defined for six, 12 and 18 months, with each party evaluating the partnership's success at each milestone. Goals could include mutual marketing programs, shared leads, joint proposals and lead-developed revenue.

Above all, successful partnerships require each party to adopt a broader mindset. As you consider future major business decisions for your company, it's good to ask yourself not only "What's in this for me?" but also "What's in it for my partner?"

Good partnering should bring your organization the equivalent of one salesperson's quota per year, every year.

16 | SELLING SUCCESSFULLY IN TOUGH TIMES

Your sales team can actually thrive during a challenging economy. Here's how.

In the economic environment we've faced in recent years, it's especially easy for salespeople to get distracted—just when it's most important to keep them focused on the steps they must take to achieve your organization's goals. At the same time, the downturn offers an exciting chance to improve your sales team's performance and increase market share as your competitors fall behind.

Motivate, Review, Analyze, Recruit, Evaluate

Acumen recommends the following 10 tactics to help your team not only make it through tough economic times, but to actually profit as well:

1. **Build the right kind of motivation.** Assess your sales-people's attitudes, then take steps to improve their focus and boost their motivation. Help build their belief in your company and what it sells by providing them with reference letters from satisfied customers, or by having those customers visit your offices to share their experiences with your entire sales organization. Make sales meetings

fun as well as productive. Hold contests and games designed to encourage team members to focus on increasing opportunities and moving business through the sales pipeline. Determine what types of incentives your salespeople like best; then tailor your rewards to those preferences.

2. **Review prices and features for all your offerings.** This is the perfect time to make sure that you're capitalizing on your strengths and meeting — or, preferably, beating — what the competition offers. Examine the existing profit margins and sales-cycle length for each product and service line. Make short-term adjustments as needed to boost revenues and margins. Revamp your existing features or offerings and consider repackaging or creating new offerings. Those steps can help confuse your competitors while developing new added-value opportunities for your company. Find ways to be different!

3. **Analyze sales and distribution channels for your markets.** First, identify the factors necessary to maximize sales. Then determine whether you're most likely to achieve your goals via a direct-sales organization, a channel-partner structure, telesales or a combination.

   Next, establish a customer focus group and ask its participants how you can best serve and support them. Finally, create a separate customer user group with regular scheduled meetings. Members of this group benefit from learning more about your products and services, and they may serve as a built-in audience for additional sales.

4. **Maintain a strong hiring pipeline.** The downturn is also a great time to ramp up your recruiting efforts. We've

found that, in today's climate, sales managers should expect to spend 25 percent of their time interviewing potential hires. The reason? Many highly qualified salespeople are seeking new opportunities right now, and it's important to keep tabs on the brightest stars.

To help focus your hiring efforts, list the five attributes you consider most important in your salespeople, then use those as guidelines for continuing to build a high-quality team. Remember, interviewing candidates doesn't necessarily mean you have to hire them. And your goal should always be to go after the top talent — not just the "best available."

5. **Evaluate and set strategy for each sales opportunity.** In an environment of intense competition and shrinking budgets, it's especially important to spend time helping salespeople think through each near-term sales opportunity. Use commercial or internally developed tools to analyze the status of each opportunity and develop strategies for increasing your probability of success. Specifically:

   • Pinpoint the prospect's likely objections; develop ways to counter them

   • Determine the buyer's decision criteria

   • Identify the decision makers and other key players

   • Initiate multi-level contact with those key players

Reach Out, Revisit and Plan

6. **Seek outside influencers to recommend what you're selling.** Third-party individuals and organizations may be able to help influence your potential customers'

decision-making processes. Potential influencers might include consultants working in the same market or with the same prospect base, or sales teams from companies that might benefit directly or indirectly from the sale of your product or service. Establish ways to identify such influencers, then create campaigns to introduce them to your company and secure their commitment to working with you.

7. **Launch an aggressive initiative to generate new sales leads.** Create a smart campaign, not a "blast" or mass-appeal plan. First, establish profiles of your current clients, listing five or so reasons why they use your products or services.

   Second, develop a strong, clear message, preferably focusing on today's key concerns: return on investment and productivity gains. Recognize that you need different messages for the CEO, the CFO and the vice presidents of sales, marketing and human resources. Modify your message based on the role of the person you're trying to reach.

   Finally, establish an action plan for the next six months — and be sure to establish a timetable for following up. Each person now needs to be "touched," or contacted, eight to 10 times a year.

8. **Revisit your compensation structure.** Clearly document your current compensation plan, tabulating payments against results over time. Is the plan achieving your original goals? Is it reinforcing the level of sales activity that you want? If not, develop a new plan, making sure that you gain buy-in from everyone on your team. Commit to keeping the new plan in place for at least six months.

Use the current market environment as an opportunity to focus on short-term goals and achievements. To try our free sales compensation assessment, visit our Web site at www.acumenmanagement.com.

9. **Contact every customer.** A downturn is also an excellent time to touch base with each of your customers. Make sure that you fully understand what clients need and how they use your products and services, then offer them new packages or deals. Or take the opportunity to obtain customer references that you can provide to potential new clients. Preplan your meeting so that you know which of your products and services these customers are already using, then determine what else you might provide to them.

   After each contact, be sure to update your customer database with any new information. Consider establishing a permanent program for periodically contacting all targeted clients, prospects, influencers and partners and reviewing what you've found during your regular sales meeting.

10. **Plan, plan, plan.** Careful planning can go a long way toward improving any sales team's effectiveness. Start by specifically defining all the steps in your sales process and determine how well each team member is executing on those steps. Then develop detailed business plans for each salesperson and create tactical plans for your key strategic accounts.

    Finally, follow up at the end of each month to determine how well each of your salespeople did in meeting the goals in their individual plans. Be ready to invest in additional training as needed.

Any economic downturn is certainly challenging, but it's not necessarily all bad news—and it won't last forever. Ultimately, these 10 tactics can help you take advantage of what we at Acumen view as the opportunity of a lifetime, during the lifetime of that opportunity.

17 | MEASURING SALES SUCCESS

The right combination of metrics can help you quickly gauge your sales team's performance and progress toward meeting your organization's goals.

In any economic environment, the companies most likely to thrive are those that take time to scrutinize their strategic sales-management plans.

These success-oriented organizations review everything from their forecasts to their pipelines, looking hard at important numbers such as cost of sales, percentage of market share, salesperson-effectiveness ratios and customer lifetime value. However, they're not just examining the numbers; they're also looking for ways to improve results based upon their chosen metrics.

We often see companies struggling because they lack such blueprints. Effective plans require combining an organization's goals and individual salespeople's business plans with a set of metrics designed to gauge everyone's progress in meeting those objectives.

The following are what we believe are the fundamental metrics that companies should include in "dashboards" for measuring their sales teams' effectiveness:

- Forecasts accuracy percentage for monthly forecast, by salesperson
- Dollar value of pipeline by stage; number of opportunities by stage
- Dollar value of pipeline ratio to future monthly quotas
- Actual sales activity compared to a defined set of standards
- Average order value by salesperson
- Win-loss rate percentages, by salesperson

Beyond the Basics

As you continue developing your company's dashboard, you may wish to build in additional metrics such as the following:

- Value of net new account sales as percentage of total sales for month and year to date
- Existing account sales as percentage of total sales, month and year to date
- Salesperson profitability as compared to sales volume
- Revenue per current customer per year as percentage of total sales
- Cost per lead, by lead source
- Number of leads, by lead source
- Close ratio by lead source
- Sales-cycle time from initial contact by salesperson to decision
- Number of days with sales outstanding, goal vs. actual
- Blended billing consultant rate, goal vs. actual
- Realization consultant rate, goal vs. actual

- Utilization consultant rate, goal vs. actual
- Consultant backlog days, goal vs. actual
- Direct sales expense as a percentage of volume, margin and quota

Looking Ahead: Leading Indicators

In addition, smart companies increasingly rely on what we call "leading indicators." These are activities or ratios that can predict revenues at least 60 days out. While simply looking at future pipeline values can provide a similar forecast, growth-focused partners may find these indicators useful as well.

In most cases, sales events occurring early in the sales cycle are most likely to lead to high-percentage sales opportunities. If these begin to fall, future pipelines and revenues will probably follow the same pattern. Potential leading indicators include the numbers of:

- New-prospect calls made per week
- Face-to-face sales calls made per week
- Subject-matter expert or pre-sales tech-support calls made per week
- Discovery calls made per month
- Demonstrations and executive presentations made per month

We also recommend creating graphs comparing those numbers to dollars booked or margins generated. Those comparisons can help salespeople see the relationship between indicators and results. All ratios should be published and shared with your entire sales team. Review the chapter on accountability for additional ideas.

Finally, remember that the ultimate goal is improving your ratios and results each month and each quarter—not simply tracking them. That's the real reason for developing a dashboard, and the real route to success.

18 | WEB WISE ON THE SALES SIDE

Your company Web site can serve as far more than a marketing and PR vehicle — it should be a genuine sales tool as well.

At Acumen, we believe that a company's sales and marketing teams should always work together, communicating frequently to make sure their messages are aligned (see chapter entitled "Sales and Marketing: Friends, Not Foes"). However, while many companies have invested significantly in Web sites that serve the marketing function of promoting a unique value proposition, many miss the sales side of the equation -- that is, proving that messaging to prospective customers.

For that reason, we recommend that your salespeople take prospects to visit your company's Web site at a suitable point in the sales process. This exercise is best done in a face-to-face sales call. In the case of a remote sales team, you could substitute a video tour of your office or use client case studies or video testimonials that reinforce your intended messaging. The new Flip video camcorders are great tools for quickly interviewing clients at trade shows, in their offices or at your own office. Then you can easily upload the resulting videos to your Web site for online viewing.

When taking prospects through your Web site, your salespeople should point out key benefits and, depending upon your value proposition, show proof of them as well. For example, if you sell based on "long-term commitment to your clients," then show two or three videos or testimonials from customers you've served for several years. If you're selling your commitment to a particular vertical market, then highlight your association memberships and your advisory-board members from that industry. If you're emphasizing that you're a low-cost provider, consider including an online ROI analysis.

In working with an Acumen client that used ROI justification in most sales situations, we helped design the company's Web site visit to work as part of their sales process. On the fourth step of the eight-step process, the salesperson would take the prospect through the Web site, including having the person complete an online questionnaire regarding a potential solution. The prospect's information was automatically run through a spreadsheet, which was then reviewed by the company's CFO.

Next, the CFO created a written analysis of the projected ROI. Then the salesperson delivered the CFO's results to the prospect, discussed the potential ROI and reviewed the value-proposition messaging. Finally, the salesperson closed by saying something along these lines: "I will work with you every quarter for the next two years to validate that these metrics will be achieved or to define what actions need to take place to ensure your ROI."

While the effort may sound labor-intensive, the interactive online experience, combined with the CFO's input, usually paid off by bringing the prospect closer to the company. The salesperson's closing commitment was designed to prove the company's marketing messaging, which, in turn, was likely to increase the prospect's trust and confidence in the organization. Additionally, whenever a prospect became a client, the salesperson automatically had a sales call scheduled to occur every 90 days for the next two years!

Often, marketing teams develop great value propositions and other messaging for their companies' Web sites and other materials, but the sales teams aren't trained to deliver those messages effectively. In fact, during many client engagements, we find that salespeople can't accurately or clearly express their organizations' value propositions.

For that reason, we recommend that you offer formal training, including role-playing exercises, to guarantee that your salespeople can effectively and correctly deliver your company's messages. Your salespeople should not be putting their own spin on those statements, either. Try videotaping your role-playing exercises, especially at the points where salespeople work on delivering your value proposition, to make sure they're delivering the messages accurately and consistently.

Bottom line: Your company's Web site should not only help all online visitors understand what your business does and invite them to investigate further, but also ensure that your selling process effectively proves your message to prospects and customers. By linking your value proposition to the emotions that prospects go through during the sales process and then creating an interactive online sales experience, you can increase both your sales velocity and your win rates.

19 | CRM & SALES CAREERS

Here's a look at the current state of customer-relationship management software, particularly in terms of its shortcomings in salesperson development.

Historically, sales management has been judged on achievement of predefined sales, revenue, market growth and quota or margin attainment. Each of these elements are critical and will continue to serve as a basic judgment on the effectiveness of sales management's success. But a CRM/SFA solution aimed at improving sales force productivity must take a big-picture approach to sales management.

In general, from a sales management perspective today's CRM systems focus on basic 1980s sales management fundamentals: activity management, call history and pipeline reviews. It's time to take a fresh look at new CRM components, most notably those that will help salespeople and managers improve individual salesperson development, that should be included in the next wave of software applications.

It should be surprising to any professional manager that CRM capability for developing a sales force--or even an individual salesperson — has so far been limited to basic sales-skill training programs and occasional product/service introduction programs.

A fundamental role of management is to ensure a thorough understanding of employees' needs, wants, desires and areas needing improvement. That understanding helps sales leaders succeed by working closely with their salespeople. It also helps eliminate two major causes of failure for both salespeople and managers: not knowing what's expected of them and not understanding their basic job functions.

Why isn't CRM meeting sales teams' needs? As an application, it hasn't assisted sales managers in developing their sales teams. Instead, it's simply helped them understand what's going wrong with sales production.

CRM must be elevated beyond the current marketing-driven product to one that sales leaders can use to truly build high-performance sales teams. Most current systems miss the point.

A successful sales-management system must focus on aligning the salesperson's soul with the corporate entity's goals. Today's sales teams need to be focused on their personal goals while simultaneously understanding how those goals relate to achieving corporate sales objectives. Sales leaders must understand the need for this balance and, in response, create systems that incorporate these views into their management styles and systems.

Any effective system must include a process to compare each salesperson's success ratio against the group's success rate. These sales actions or success factors are generally the four or five measurements that show proper sales-activity ratios compared against performance. These measurements should be taken weekly and monthly, graphed and reconciled with bookings and revenue attainment for the same periods. This graphing for success allows all salespeople to visualize and understand their unique activity requirements and how they can exceed their sales-achievement goals. Most important, this practice allows the sales manager to begin coaching and mentoring individual team members on their personal levels of activity for success.

The next step should be allowing each salesperson, with sales management approval, to create a personal professional-development process. CRM systems should include a set of development tools that allow--and even force-- the sales manager to regularly review each salesperson's development. These would be self-generated quarterly development tools that allow managers and salespeople to review both successes and areas needing improvement. Workflow management systems can be developed along with the appropriate tool set to manage this function.

Salesperson development programs should focus on sales development, product or service knowledge, industry expertise, company operations, technology exposure and personal growth. These areas of emphasis create a "well-rounded" approach to development rather than a one-dimensional focus on skills. Such program should be ongoing efforts, renewed every six months to ensure that they're continuing to enhance a sales organization's professionalism

CRM software programs were developed to improve sales productivity, so it's not clear why they haven't focused on creating the career paths or personal and professional development needed to achieve that objective. In many industries, professional development involves formal certification. If proof of professional development is considered important in the legal, financial, technical and educational fields, among others, why it isn't it considered critical for sales or for sales management? To date, CRM programs haven't included a set of processes or tools for taking a systematic approach to sales-team development. Yet overseeing each salesperson's development should be the fundamental focus of any sales manager interested in long-term success.

Most CRM software applications provide tools to develop

active sales strategy and tactics, but few — if any--CRM software products develop a salesperson's knowledge or thinking process in terms of determining territory planning or account development. Yet those skills are necessary to attain market/account penetration and sales achievement goals. Especially in tough economic times, it's critical to ensure that every potential sales opportunity is uncovered and worked.

The best sales managers are always remembered for not only how well they achieved sales goals, but also how they helped develop great salespeople who moved up in their own organizations or at other companies. It's time for the CRM industry to recognize that its role should include helping sales managers develop successful sales teams, not simply reporting why they failed. I like to believe sales leaders must be proactive rather than reactive.

20 | CRM, LEADERSHIP & MANAGEMENT

Some sales executives are leaders; others are managers. All need applications to help them hold salespeople accountable for achieving the company's goals and their own.

By now, it should be clear that sales management can have either a positive or negative impact on sales management. High-performing sales organizations are led by people who truly understand the role of sales management. Under-performing sales organizations typically reflect management that doesn't fully understand its role — and traditional CRM can be one ingredient in that recipe for failure.

In the previous positive economic environment, many sales organizations were overachieving not *because* of sales management, but *despite* it. In more difficult economic times, the sins of poor or ineffective sales management become obvious to everyone — especially the company's senior executive leadership and its board of directors. Achievement now hinges on building sales organizations that can succeed in tough times and excel in more positive ones.

We've found that in many of today's struggling companies, sales managers confuse leadership and management. We define leadership as *the ability to make things happen by encouraging and channeling contributions of others, taking a stand on and addressing important issues and acting as a catalyst for change and continuous improvement.*

While the entire definition is important, pay special attention to these key words and phrases: "encouraging," "taking a stand," "acting as a catalyst for change and improvement."

These are calls to action. They focus on taking a proactive stance rather than a reactive one. As part of that stance, sales leaders need to set clear standards and hold salespeople accountable for achieving them. But many fail to do this, and their inaction essentially sets the standards to the lowest achievement level of the least successful salesperson. In this situation, sales management has stopped being a catalyst for growth and continuous improvement.

In contrast, many people who hold responsibility for sales function strictly as managers. We define management as: *the skill of attaining predefined objectives with and through the cooperation and effort of other people.*

Notice the words "skill," "attaining predefined objectives." Again, while the entire definition is important, those key words spell out that management is a *skill*, meaning that it can be learned. "Attaining predefined objectives" means that someone else—a leader--has set the goals; a manager measures the results.

One typical area for sales management's failure has been its focus on pipeline management. That's because historically, a larger part of the sales manager's role has been holding salespeople accountable for pipeline values and sales. While this aspect of is important— it reflects only one aspect of successful sales organizations.

When we compare successful companies, we've found several common traits, including a strong emphasis on people and culture.

This is an area that divides ineffective sales managers from successful ones. In many cases, the problem goes back to focusing on management rather than on leadership. Failing sales managers have focused on "holding firm" on their numbers and, at worst, have allowed underachievers to survive in their organizations. In contrast, successful sales leaders have created or used management systems that focus on helping top-level and average producers succeed at greater levels.

Successful sales leaders allow the individuals to set personal goals that map to corporate goals. Sales management must approve each individual's goals, ensuring that they meet or exceed company expectations, and then coach, mentor and monitor progress towards those objectives. Bottom line: If individual salespeople don't achieve their objectives or commitments, sales management must work to correct their behavior — or terminate their employment.

To ensure success, sales management should follow these fundamental steps to build a sales organization that will achieve continuous long-term results:

- Develop and share sense of mission or purpose
- Have clear and attainable goals
- Provide frequent objective feedback
- Provide positive rewards for appropriate performance
- Give timely support and help when requested or needed

Unfortunately, most CRM applications currently don't help sales managers create an environment based on individual coaching, goal-setting or personal development.

Sales managers of all types need applications designed to assist them in holding people accountable to achieving both the company's goals and their own. Sales-management software should include, among other things, applications to help salespeople set and track their progress on those personal and company goals, their personal development plans, their networking commitments — and, yes, their quota attainment.

With or without CRM, today's sales managers must remember that setting goals and developing standards is the easy part. The real challenge is in holding salespeople accountable to their own standards and those of the company. The most important step is taking the right corrective action when those standards aren't being set and standards aren't being achieved. Recognizing and following through on that step takes leadership rather than management — and that's the most important ingredient of all for success.

PART III:

HIRING, TRAINING

&

COMPENSATION

21 | HIRING WISELY AND WELL

Don't get stuck with an empty suit! Try these five tips for finding the best salespeople for your company.

Hiring effectively is the first step in building a profitable organization — and, for just about any company — a top challenge.

If that sounds like overstatement, consider this: failure to achieve profits often relates directly to hiring salespeople who can't carry out their assigned roles — or meet their necessary goals. Many companies focus on hiring only when the need arises, a practice that results in a hiring process that isn't designed to ensure that you hire the best — not just the best available. Recruiting is a commitment; it should consume 25 percent of the sales leader's time. And the process must be as well organized as your delivery methodology.

Many companies rely on inconsistent interviewing techniques. They tend to believe what they hear and, as a result, end up hiring an "empty suit." A Michigan State University study found that more than 90 percent of all hiring decisions were made as the result of interviews, but that information gathered during interviews is frequently inaccurate.

Clearly, hiring high-quality salespeople requires using high-quality practices. Start by following these five steps:

1. **Keep your interviewing skills active.** Set a goal to interview X number of candidates per month, every month, even if you have no openings. In any sales organization, at any given time, about 20 percent of the people can be replaced. Harsh, but true.

2. **Advertise for new personnel about six times per year.** While that may sound like a lot, remember that the person you need to hire may not be looking, or may not be available when you start looking, especially if you only interview sporadically. It's important to keep your recruiting pipeline full.

3. **Set interviewing minimums for each hire.** Interview at least five candidates for each hire and involve at least three other staffers in the process. Ideally, each staffer involved in interviewing should have a different role in the organization to ensure diversity of opinion.

4. **Schedule at least one interview off-site in a social atmosphere.** For instance, consider meeting the candidate for lunch or dinner. This is especially important when the job calls for working in similar social environments. But even if that's not the case, keep in mind that candidates often open up more in a relaxed atmosphere.

5. **Make sure the sales leader manages the recruiting pipeline as seriously as the sales pipeline.** They're directly related and equally important. To assess the candidates in your pipeline, define five specific, objective, measurable experiences or characteristics for your ideal salesperson. Why so few? Because it's important to zero in on areas that drive success. The criteria will differ depending on the exact position, but should be as simple as this example:

   • At least five years of sales experience
   • Experience in opening new territories or new accounts

- Regional sales experience
- Expertise in a specific market or industry
- Professional sales training

It's important to make this profile document available to everyone involved in the interview process, including recruiting firms. Use it for writing your help-wanted postings, too.

Strive for Consistency

Now that you have a plan to fill the pipeline with quality candidates, the next step is to systemize the process for selecting the right ones Spelling out the process to everyone involved not only saves time, but provides candidates with a unified professional view of your company, increasing their desire to join the sales team.

The following model consistently works well. Consider adopting it as a foundation for your sales-recruitment process:

1. Identify and document each stage in the interview process, and decide who in your company will participate.

2. Use a proven assessment tool or test with your top sales representatives and a few of your less-successful junior team members. These online tests can provide a benchmark for evaluating candidates' sales abilities, mental strength and attitudes toward selling. Sales assessments provide information into candidates that you can't necessarily glean from in-person interviews. They can also provide valuable management insights about candidates that you end up hiring.

3. Distribute the following information to all your company

interview participants:

- Outline of the interview process
- Profile of the ideal sales candidate
- Interviewing scorecard
- List of basic questions to ask
- Each candidate's resume
- Scenarios for testing candidates' sales knowledge

No question: Building a recruiting process takes effort. So does ensuring that everyone follows the plan. But the result—the creation of a winning sales team—is guaranteed to make life less stressful and more productive for any sales leader.

For more detailed information on recruiting, interviewing and on-boarding, *The Sales Management Guru's Guide: Recruiting High Performance Sales Teams,* will provide you with tips, tools, and ideas on interviewing, questioning, and training. Go to www.AcumenManagement.com.

22 | TEN TRAITS OF SALES SUPERSTARS

Selling yourself is just the first step. You've also got to demonstrate deep knowledge, provide valuable resources make the buyer look great.

What *really* separates the best salespeople from the rest of the pack? Acumen's research shows that top performers not only understand each prospect's company extremely well— they understand the person making the buying decisions as well.

Most sales-training courses emphasize the importance of addressing the customer's needs. They teach salespeople to explain how a particular product or service can help achieve key business goals. Certainly, those discussions are critical for making sales.

But too few training programs address how buyers view salespeople as they're presenting that information —knowledge that can be an equally powerful sales tool.

How Sales Superstars Work with Buyers

Our research indicates that, from the buyer's point of view, the best salespeople:

1. **Listen.** Buyers want to deal with professionals who ask the right questions and truly listen to the answers. They want to work with salespeople who can take what they've heard and translate it into appropriate solutions. Want to boost your listening skills to top-performer level? Take notes, summarize and restate what buyers tell you and, equally important, *listen* when they confirm whether you've gotten it right.

2. **Tell the truth.** I cringe when I hear salespeople tell customers or prospects, "Let me be honest with you," as if they haven't been honest so far. If you don't know the answer, don't make it up. If you aren't professional enough to sell without lying, find a new profession.

3. **Do more than push products/services.** Of course, it's vitally important for salespeople to know about the products/services they represent, but talking only about features and functions went out in the '70s. Today's top performers focus on helping buyers achieve their business goals. One way to do that: Videotape and watch your own sales presentation to see from the buyer's point of view. Are you helping — or just selling? Another hint: make a sales call without samples or product information and see how the conversation changes or how dependent you are on them.

4. **Know each customer's business.** Going after vertical markets has become a major emphasis for many companies in recent years, selling into a vertical market requires you KNOW the industry, but even in a horizontal market you must take the time to learn their business. Stay abreast of — or even ahead of — developments in your customers' worlds. When prospects see that you're familiar with their businesses and industries, you'll gain their trust and confidence , which are key ingredients in any successful sales formula. Guru Hint: check out your prospects' national association web sites.

5. **Know what each customer's clients need.** The real Pro's seek to understand their prospects customer's needs. See No. 4.

6. **Address pain points.** Top performers outdo the competition by personalizing their presentations to show how whatever they're selling will help customers resolve specific business problems, achieve important goals and generate impressive ROI. Keep it simple and straight forward.

7. **Keep promises.** Buyers keep track of what you say, you do and whether you actually do it. If you offer to send a white paper or list of references, follow through. And get it there when promised — never request an extension.

8. **Avoid wasting time.** As a salesperson, you've got the right to be persistent and to be respected, but not to be a pest. Dropping in unannounced because you were "in the neighborhood" falls into the latter category; it's also the mark of an amateur. Instead, schedule your calls, have a stated objective for each meeting and be sure the time you use results in value for the customer.

9. **Serve as an information resource.** Top-performing salespeople often provide customers with useful background materials, typically from reputable outside sources. Consider passing along relevant information from *The Wall Street Journal*, local business journals, industry magazines or credible e-newsletters, Web sites or blogs.

10. **Make the buyer a hero.** Top performers always know what personal factors drive each buyer's behavior, whether it's ego, desire for a bonus, the potential for promotion or another factor. Do what's necessary to make sure your important buyers regard a particular sales as a personal wins. Reinforce this subtly.

Long ago, someone told me the three key factors in sales are: emotion, emotion, emotion. No question about it: If you recognize your buyers' emotions, you'll accelerate your sales.

23 | THE ESSENCE OF EDUCATION

Developing well-coordinated training programs for new salespeople and existing salespeople alike can provide tremendous ROI.

In working with clients, we at Acumen Management often find that sales-training programs suffer from problems such as inadequate new-employee orientation, sporadic and unfocused ongoing training and nonexistent or ineffective role-playing scenarios. Many clients also lack any type of coaching or mentoring in the field, during or after routine sales calls.

The good news: sales training programs don't have to be sophisticated or expensive. To ensure success, you need only a few basic components: a comprehensive plan that spells out your training program's goals and components, a clear ongoing process and, above all, effective execution.

A Comprehensive Plan

Your plan should contain an outline for initial employee training on functional job requirements, company product and service offerings and corporate benefits, along with recurring plans for training existing employees.

Many organizations' training plans are missing one key factor: making sure that employee interest and motivation levels remain high. This process, which involves helping team members commit to the organization and align their personal and professional interests, is known as "re-recruiting."

The perfect opportunity to set a lasting tone is when new employees join your company. If you have customer letters of reference, have the newcomers read them. If you have awards, explain how you earned them. All new employees should have lunch or a meeting with the person at the highest level in their divisions; in smaller companies, that would be the president. Commitment, loyalty and the right attitude will begin to develop at these sessions.

At Acumen, we believe in creating a detailed three-week new-hire training plan. Each week is broken down into specific training and knowledge-transfer components— with homework! The plan must cover everything, including:

- Legal documents
- Marketing case studies
- Using the phone, fax machine and customer relationship management (CRM) system
- Presenting and selling your organization via its brochures and PowerPoint presentations
- Scheduled lunch meetings with key executives

… and more, based on your organization's specific needs.

It's critical that you clearly define each element of your training program and that the people responsible for each area sign off as each new hire has successfully completed the training.

We have included a sample of the three-week new hire training plan in *The Sales Management Guru's Guide: Recruiting High Performance Sales Teams.*

A Clear Long-Term Process

To ensure success, your training plan should be designed so that you're continually updating your team's abilities. The plan should cover the following areas: sales skills, product and services knowledge, company operations, industry awareness and, if appropriate, understanding of key vertical markets.

Plan and organize your sales meetings for the entire quarter. Develop a comprehensive plan for repeatedly touching on each of the elements listed above over the course of the quarter (although not necessarily addressing all of them at each event).

The plan should also include personalized six-month programs that allow salespeople to set their own goals. This process helps ensure that individual and corporate goals are fully aligned. One of my clients requires its salespeople to attain several certification levels each year. In one instance, the salesperson has 15 minutes to review a case study before walking into a room where an actor plays the role of the client. Three independent professionals evaluate the salesperson's performance, which may be videotaped for later review. The salesperson must receive a passing grade before moving on to the next level.

Effective Execution

To get your training program off the ground, first develop a written three-month sales training plan. Include a mandatory, predefined schedule; emphasize that employees must schedule their other meetings around the meeting schedule. Assign sales team members to present most training topics (if salespeople have to train others on a topic, you can be sure they'll know the material cold). Schedule sessions with out-side trainers at least once per quarter. Establishing a short-term plan and agenda ensures that you address current issues while meeting the goals for providing ongoing training.

Bottom line: Employees are a critical asset. Most software systems have regular maintenance check-ups and support agreements to keep them at current levels. Your employees require at least as much attention. Keeping your employees' personal and professional objectives aligned with your cor-porate goals through training and re-recruiting will ultimate-ly result in huge dividends.

24 | INVEST IN YOURSELF

Creating your own annual training "curriculum" can help you excel, year after year.

Not long ago, I read an article that emphasized the importance of annually reviewing your various investment plans. That advice brought to mind a practice of many salespeople I've met over the past decade. As they conduct their year-end reviews, they look at their year-to-date earnings and say to themselves, "Am I where I want to be?"

But in doing those self-evaluations, salespeople often forget to consider one important factor: how well, or whether, they've invested in their own professional growth.

In sales, as in most other fields, what distinguishes the professionals from the amateurs is a high-level combination of education, expertise and dedication. So in undertaking their annual self-assessments, serious salespeople should evaluate not only their numbers, but what they've done to enhance their commitment to their profession by improving their knowledge and skills.

The best in the business consciously strive to increase their value by investing in themselves. To follow their lead, try these professional-development activities:

Read good general-business books. Many executives read business bestsellers. Doing the same will provide you with fresh insights that you can discuss with prospects and customers. Increased business acumen can strengthen relationships by generating new levels of respect—which also further differentiates you from the competition. As a rule, I recommend reading at least two business books a year. (Guru Hint: If you're on the road a lot, consider subscribing to services that provide audio books.)

Read sales-training books. When I interview prospective sales candidates for our clients, I always ask about the last sales-training book they read and how long ago they read it. The answer provides a sure sign of the candidate's level of commitment to the sales profession. Look for guides focusing on strategy, complex sales, solutions and negotiation tactics.

We often recommend having your entire sales team read the same sales training book. Assign different salespeople to report on different chapters each week. In their reports, team members should highlight the important factors in "their" chapters, relating the key points to specific aspects of your business. The entire team can participate in the resulting discussion.

We also recommend establishing a sales-training library and stocking it with relevant books, CDs and industry information. You might also want to follow the lead of some of our other clients, who created sales-certification programs for evaluating each employee's progress in acquiring new knowledge every year.

Subscribe to relevant business and technology magazines and newsletters. This ongoing reading program will keep you up to date on important business and technology issues and trends ---- as long as you actually *read* the publications.

As a sales manager, I typically assigned specific magazines to certain salespeople. As described above, they were responsible for highlighting pertinent information and reporting on their findings during sales meetings. We also attached lists of team members to each magazine's cover so people could check off their names after reading and passing along the publication. (I read these publications while relaxing and have even carried them along to the beach in the summer; I consider this professional-development time.)

Meanwhile, don't forget to read newspapers and online content offered by The Wall Street Journal or other news organizations.

Practice for perfection. Professionals in every field get ready for important events. Musicians rehearse. Baseball players go through spring training. Salespeople should prepare as well.

Before every sales call, plan your entire approach. If you're making sales calls with your colleagues, be sure everyone understands who's leading the discussion, when other participants will present and who's playing on the prospect's team.

For especially important calls, consider working with other salespeople ahead of time to role-play your approach for handling objections or discuss your ideas for closing. If you haven't videotaped your sales presentation in two years or more, it's time for an encore and, possibly some additional practice. Finally, rehearse your verbal skills as well. Call your own phone and leave a voice message. Then play it back and try to evaluate it objectively. Would *you* return the call?

Analyze your own performance. Professional football players study post-game films; professional salespeople should take a similar approach to assess how well they've performed. In fact, this is the most important step in professional self-development—fortunately, it's also the easiest.

Train yourself to review *every* sales call you make, whether it's a phone call, a face-to-face meeting, a presentation or a demonstration. Simply ask yourself, "If I could do it over again, what—if anything--would I do differently?" Sales leaders should encourage such self-examination at every opportunity: That question is the first step toward a self-managed sales team (see the separate chapter on how to build such teams).

One last note: Be sure to leverage your vendor relations for additional training resources. Many vendors offer not only product knowledge training but related sales-skills training as well.

I challenge you to evaluate your professional growth from the past year, then develop a game plan for investing in yourself during the next year. Your efforts are likely to pay off, literally, in higher earnings. Meanwhile, if you'd like more specific suggestions about useful books, magazines and newsletters, e-mail me at ken@acumenmgmt.com and I'll send you our list of recommended resources.

25 | THE ART OF DISCOVERY

Salespeople must do more than asking the right questions—they must also understand the answers from the prospect's perspective.

In the past couple of years, I've heard a lot about the importance of building a solutions-based practice, understanding the prospect's pain and becoming a trusted business advisor. Those are all genuine needs and critical elements for sales success.

At the same time, these concepts are nothing new. In fact, they're the same ones that I learned when entering the profession more than 25 years ago. I believe that where we should be focusing instead-—especially in terms of training—is the art of discovery.

The art of discovery involves more than just asking basic qualifying questions, such as: "Who is making the decision?" "When are you making the decision?" and "Has your budget been defined?"

It even goes beyond asking more in-depth questions, such as: "How is your organization positioned for the future both from an IT perspective and in terms of competition?" and "How will the mergers and acquisitions in your industry affect your business?"

The Prospect's Point of View

Simply put, the art of discovery involves teaching salespeople — both in the office and in the field — how to "connect the dots." This means that salespeople must know not only how to ask the right questions, but also to understand the answers from a prospect's perspective.

Most important, they must know how to respond. They must know how to ask the proper follow-up questions and probe further based on their own analysis of what they're hearing. Skilled salespeople can then connect those comments to descriptions of how their company's solutions can address the challenges, problems or needs that they've uncovered.

Too often, we observe salespeople "winging it" when they meet with potential customers — that is, arriving without prepared questions and failing to take notes during the meeting. That's a serious mistake. Thoughtful questions and detailed notes are essential to the art of discovery.

Practice and Review

The best way to teach salespeople to connect the dots is through role-playing, preferably with videotaped exercises. We recommend setting up a "sales call" in the office and role-playing it with good questions and realistic customer responses. This practice allows salespeople to formally rehearse how they should respond.

But the real win comes from having them review the exercise on videotape, where they can really see, hear and begin to adjust their performances. Allowing other sales team members to watch the video will help them learn as well by illustrating what works and what doesn't.

For one Acumen client, we developed a certification process in which salespeople had 15 minutes to read a case study and then make a sales call on a "prospect," who was actually a professional actor who had been given a slightly different scenario. We then assigned a panel of three observers to judge each sales call using a pass-fail grading system. That kind of pressure, backed with proper pre-exercise training, is the secret to teaching salespeople to connect the dots when they're in front of a qualified prospect. It's also a great way to position them for high-level performance.

To build an ongoing training system, we recommend that you keep videotapes of the top performances and replay them often. To obtain ongoing benefits from practicing the art of discovery, periodically change the questions in your case studies to better reflect the current situations that your team is facing.

Spend time in your sales meetings creating a "best-questions" list. Questions on the list should be open-ended, strategic and worded specifically for your products and services. Update your best-questions list regularly and use it during training as well as on sales calls in the field.

Then just watch your win-loss ratios improve, your pipeline velocity increase and your overall sales go up!

26 | PRE-CALL PREP

These steps can help ensure that you're as ready as possible for that all-important sales call.

As a rookie salesperson, I learned that when it comes to making sales calls, it's best to follow the Boy Scout motto: Be prepared.

Back then, a sales manager and I once drove 45 miles to see one of my early-stage prospects. Along the way, we talked about sports, our past jobs and life in general. When we arrived at our destination, I started to get out of the car. Then, suddenly, the manager fired a series of questions at me: "What's the purpose of this visit? How will you open the call? What's your desired outcome?" After I stammered a few non-answers, we closed the car doors and began to strategize.

That embarrassing experience taught me a valuable lesson: Every successful sales call requires focus and preparation. In that case, for instance, we could have used that 45-minute drive to consider our tactics and generate creative approaches. Since then, I've taken pains to prepare for every sales call, whether it's in person or by telephone.

Steps for Pre-Call Prep

Here are eight steps I recommend that all salespeople take before meeting with prospects or customers:

1. **Know the objective.** Be able to answer questions such as: What outcome do I want? How will I direct the discussion to make sure that I reach my desired goal?

2. **Prepare questions.** Before every meeting, write down lists of technical and business questions that can help guide the conversation. Refer to these lists during the sales call and take notes on those all-important answers.

3. **Prepare answers.** Anticipate any tough questions and potential objections. Develop and polish the best possible answers and responses. Role-play possible scenarios with your manager or other salespeople.

4. **Do your homework.** Start by mining your own files or customer-relationship management (CRM) database for information about a prospect or customer. Then learn as much as you can about the company from its Web site, including reading its online press releases describing new activities and personnel changes. If possible, obtain and study an organization chart. Explore industry and competitor Web sites for additional insights about the company's value proposition and place in its industry. The better you understand any organization, the more likely you are to become one of its trusted business advisors.

5. **Have a game plan.** Determine the seating sequence and roles of all participants in the sales call or visit. If possible, mix up participant seating. Try to avoid having your entire team on one side and all the prospects on the other. Make sure everyone on your team understands who opens, who delivers, who closes and who answers what types of questions. Equally important: Make sure everyone knows what issues or topics to avoid.

6. **Rehearse your opening.** Consider role-playing your client greeting and your non-business "ice-breaker." That's important because stumbling early with awkward conversation will limit your ability to control the call. You may want to consider recapping the purpose of your call and your agreed-upon time limit. I like to also ask: <u>"Has anything changed since our last meeting?"</u>

7. **Bring the right information.** Make sure you've got the correct brochures, data sheets and other materials. If you're presenting or demonstrating a product , don't forget to provide the right supporting documents. Make sure you check your computer, projector and other systems beforehand to make sure everything's working properly. Do you have a backup plan if something fails?

8. **Plan your closing.** Know how you'll wind up the session, including establishing next steps. Always set the date for the next meeting, before you leave.

One major rule of professional selling is: Always leave a task for the other party to complete. Why? Because as you walk out the door, another salesperson will walk in or a new business problem will pop up and your potential buyers will immediately begin to forget what you just discussed. Leave your prospects with action items, which can be as minor as sending you additional information or as major as scheduling people for your next meeting.

Whether you're a salesperson or an executive, I recommend bringing up these issues at your next sales meeting. At the very least, being well prepared for sales calls can help you avoid repeating my early embarrassing experience. But beyond that, it's a good way to demonstrate true commitment to the profession. And being a true pro is, of course, a great way to differentiate yourself in the marketplace.

27 | BRINGING PERSONALITY TO SALES

Approaching buyers based on their individual personality types can help you build relationships and close deals.

Typically, buyers fit into one of four main personality types. Knowing buyers' styles can help you communicate better with each one — and increase sales volume and velocity as a result.

Following are the most common personality styles that you might encounter, along with advice on selling to each of them.

Directors

A Director has a get-to-the-point style and stays focused on the job. Relationships aren't important to this personality type. When dealing with Directors, emphasize the short-term benefits of what you're selling and appeal to the Director's need to gain the advantage.

Briefly cover the main benefits of your products or services. Isolate the dollar-related topics or verifiable benefits. Keep alert for signs of impatience. In presentations, use brief, bottom-line visuals and ask open-ended questions designed to make the prospect talk. Allow the director to lead.

To speed up closing with a Director, provide alternatives, handle objections by taking issue with the facts and not the person, and focus on objectives, results and a sense of urgency. Finally, ask for the order. Be dramatic and brief, then be quiet.

Persuaders

A Persuader is outgoing and expressive and wants to be the center of attention. Approach a Persuader informally, using the person's first name. Listen for clues to personal information such as details about the Persuader's family or interests; converse about those topics as you develop a relationship.

Avoid formal visuals and PowerPoint presentations. Instead, use handouts with testimonial information that's woven into an interesting, unstructured discussion. Show respect by being open and honest, even when it comes to talking about the weaknesses of your products or services

In closing, provide examples of solutions accepted by others whom the Persuader respects. Offer incentives for the Persuader's willingness to take a risk. Speak to the Persuader's dreams; make the person a hero. Create a sense of urgency that helps persuade the Persuader to buy—but don't make the close too obvious. Focus on next steps and use an assumptive close by providing ideas for taking action.

Analysts

Analytical personality types are organizational record-keepers, but don't assume that they only hold the roles of CFO or controller. Executives in many other specialty areas can be analytical as well.

Analysts will be skeptical and especially wary of exaggerated claims. During your sales process, you'll need to emphasize research that supports your points. Know the client's situation thoroughly. Be ready to state facts and prepare alternative choices.

Your discussion must be detailed, logical and low key. Emphasize the tested, proven and well-documented aspects of your implementation process and probe for issues that might be barriers. With Analytical buyers, your presentations should include visuals, charts and statistics that can be left behind for review. Make no mistake: these documents will be read.

During your closing with Analytical types, it's important to be thorough. If you can't get a commitment, ask for specific next steps. Restate your summary and those newly provided next steps as a trial close before ending the meeting.

Supporters

In working with Supporters, it's important to realize your role in their decision-making process. As a professional, you'll need to research a client's growth plans and show how your solution will benefit the client company.

In your sales call, ask open-ended questions that reveal future and current plans. Then relate how your solution benefits those plans. In conversation, allow some latitude to give Supporter clients opportunities to open up and express their feelings.

During your presentation, think laterally. Use the Supporter as a sounding board; invite his or her comments on the plans. But be careful not to push or crowd. You must build trust and convey respect by recognizing the Supporter's achievements and intelligence. Supporters prefer cooperation and stability over confrontation.

During your closing, provide Supporters with examples

of others who have accepted what you're selling. Use a low-key, assumptive close to assist them with their goals. Avoid hard, "ask-for-order" selling; instead, help Supporters make positive decisions. Selling trust and confidence is critical here.

People are complicated. Everyone has a portion of each of the four personality structures, but most people often have one dominant style and a secondary style. The more you know about each prospect's personality style, and the better you understand how to work with each type, the more likely you are to build relationships that result in sales.

In a complex sale involving multiple decision makers or recommenders, you will have multiple personality styles to address. Make sure that your presentations include portions that address each personality type.

28 | SALES MANAGEMENT: THE FINAL FRONTIER

Sales organizations are under more pressure from top management than ever before, and that's not likely to change soon. Here's how to stand up to scrutiny and prepare for the future.

Sales management has never really been analyzed like other areas of business. CEOs have strengthened balance sheets with better asset management, reduced inventory and cost levels with just-in-time methodology, and increased direct-mail and advertising effectiveness with testing and reporting methods. Now, with increased pressure to reduce costs and enhance productivity, the focus has shifted to sales. That shift has profound implications for the sales organization and sales management.

The Evolving Sales Role

The role of sales must change because buyers are becoming more sophisticated. In addition, there's less differentiation among products and services and companies are facing a greater need to cut costs. The internet has leveled the ground from a knowledge perspective and in some industry's from a buying mode. As a result, company leadership is scrutinizing strategic sales management, sales productivity, pipeline or forecasting accuracy, dollar values, cost of sales, market share, sales process, customer lifetime values and salesperson effectiveness more than ever before. All organizations -- whether their revenues are stalled or growing -- face increased pressure to create a sales-distribution organization that generates consistent, profitable results.

Sales jobs are changing as well. In the future, there will be more outsourcing of certain sales functions, such as lead-generation activities. The role of sales is also being stratified, meaning that instead of just having one salesperson, there could be several salespeople with specific functions such as pre-sales, technical sales and post-sales.

Technology is another catalyst for change. New technology tools can help salespeople demonstrate products online, track prospects and improve customer service — all while cutting costs as the same time allowing prospects and customers greater access to company, product or service solutions.

Manufacturing environments face a focus on quality, cost control and performance measurement. Accounting focuses on audit, controls, execution and performance. But in many sales organizations, we find a lack of performance standards, little or no business planning, frightening turnover levels and compensation plans that aren't aligned to corporate strategies.

Building a Better Sales Team

Following are 10 tactics for building a sales organization that's more effective and better prepared for top-level scrutiny — and for the future:

1. Visit your most satisfied customers to find out why they purchased from you and why they stay with you.

2. Review your products, services and pricing. Are they competitive? Are they unique?

3. Analyze how your sales team can best serve customers. Build a new philosophy.

4. Muscle up your sales team. Hire the best person for each job. Recruit constantly, even when you don't need to fill vacancies immediately.

5. Carefully analyze each sales opportunity. Strategize more carefully and involve multiple people.

6. Identify supporters who will recommend your products and services. Find leverage points to grow sales.

7. Create new leads with an active target-marketing campaign. Build a rolling six-month marketing calendar of events.

8. Review your current compensation plan. Does it meet your strategic objectives?

9. Increase your investment in sales skills and product/service knowledge. Plan a 90-day sales-training event each quarter.

10. Connect all clients who purchased something from your organization in the past 12 months. Determine what else you might sell them.

Finally, remember that failing to plan is the No. 1 obstacle to revenue generation. Effective planning can dramatically increase your chances for success in all those areas.

29 | A FRESH LOOK AT CERTIFICATION

Creating your own sales-certification program can result in lower turnover, improved recruiting ability, stronger customer relationships and wider recognition in your industry.

Professional organizations in many industries long ago recognized the importance of creating ways to increase practitioners' knowledge and expertise. As a result, those industries require professionals to obtain a certain number of Continuing Education Units (CEUs) each year, and many organizations offer ongoing training programs to ensure that professionals constantly continue updating their knowledge and skills.

These credentials play a critical role in delivering the services that drive most organizations. They were also designed to help professionals in a many fields perform more effectively while offering them the chance to differentiate themselves to clients based on their continuing-education achievements. This approach is common practice in the legal, engineering, accounting, information technology and financial industries, among others.

In today's economy, business development and customer relationship management have become boardroom issues. Having a well-trained sales organization is especially critical to meeting those top-level expectations.

The current challenge for both U.S. and worldwide business is to build or gain market share while retaining existing customers. Increasing requirements for growing revenues, maintaining predictable revenue, creating differentiation and lowering cost of sales have prompted organizations to consider building certification levels into the sales team's professional development plans.

In the past, business has focused on quality, just-in-time inventory, branding, mission statements and technology to assist in creating an efficient, effective and more productive organization. At Acumen, we're finding that sales management now receives more scrutiny than ever from executive leaders, with strong emphasis on improving how salespeople deliver the company's messages, services and products. Sales certification is becoming the cornerstone of those efforts— and an important factor in helping companies differentiate themselves increasingly crowded marketplaces.

In addition, customers are demanding solution-oriented approaches that are personalized to their own requirements. While sales training does address some of those issues, it typically lacks formal recognition for salespeople who have acquired the levels of expertise required of today's top professionals.

In highly competitive markets, salespeople must fully understand multi-level sales skills, product and service offerings, industry expertise, client industry knowledge, competitive market offerings and personal career development skills. A fully developed certification program will cover those areas for team members at every stage of their careers.

Why Do It?

Creating a certification program can reap enormous benefits:

lower turnover, improved recruiting ability, stronger customer relationships and wider recognition in your industry. Today's end users want salespeople to be consultative, serving as trusted resources. Unfortunately, most sales organizations still focus primarily on selling products and services and achieving sales quotas.

One study of the top 10 U.S. sales organizations found the following common characteristics:

1. Sales effectiveness is essential.
2. Business strategies come first.
3. The best sales practices are consistent from industry to industry.
4. The sales organization is a corporate priority; sales is a highly valued career.
5. Structured sales process is key to success.
6. Team sales prevail.
7. Recruitment and training are critically important.
8. Sales compensation is linked to corporate objectives.
9. Corporate image and branding are important to sales.
10. Corporate culture is deep and consistent.

These basic findings highlight the need for an effective new approach to managing a sales organization. Sales management and team members may believe in—and even put into practice—those key attributes, but certification programs provide a formal way for making sure everything is linked, tested, verified and delivered.

Ensuring success also requires not just those essential elements, but an ongoing program that builds belief in your company and its products and services while verifying that your sales representatives know everything they need to know. Certification programs will create a focused, skilled, high-performance sales team that can help differentiate your organization from the competition.

What are the fundamental ingredients to building a certification program for your organization?

First, obviously, is commitment. A certification program should be viewed not just a new training initiative but as a permanent process emphasizing achievement. It should be designed into overall efforts to develop career paths, and it must have the support of all senior executives inside and outside the sales organization. It requires an ongoing financial commitment as well.

Second, the program must be carefully developed and rolled out, then regularly enhanced and updated. Certification levels and achievement and program content should be aligned to your particular company as well as to market and industry trends.

Third, the certification program must be initiated across the board, from beginning salespeople to top-performing veterans. Senior sales executives should be involved in the program's creation, implementation and ongoing execution, and certification should be part of their own professional development. Peer involvement, peer approval and performance evaluations are all key ingredients.

Certified salespeople must master each area covered in the program, then regularly continue enhancing and updating their skills and knowledge.

A baseline sales certification program should cover the following factors:

- Company mission, vision, message, value proposition and goals for success. This section builds belief in the company and its products and services.

- Company internal processes and operations. This section explains how and why your organization does what it does, how CRM works and so on.
- Understanding your company's industry. This section provides understanding of key components, trends, regulations and issues.
- Understanding the client's business. This section goes beyond a simple overview to providing a solid understanding of the client's strategy, market, value proposition, competition and finances.
- Understanding the client's industry. Again, this section covers key components, trends and issues.
- Sales skills. This section includes:

    ◊ Resolution process
    ◊ Presentation skills
    ◊ Account and territory strategy and tactics
    ◊ Sales techniques
    ◊ Forecasting
    ◊ Technology
    ◊ Sales tools

Each section should be designed with self-study material, case studies, role-playing and client peer review. Course material should be as realistic as possible. Be sure to include a thorough evaluation process for determining how well each salesperson has mastered the information. It's also critical to include a scoring system designed to set the level of performance expectation. You might also consider recording or videotaping the role-playing exercises so that salespeople can view their actual performances.

During each six-month period, salespeople should submit to both management and to a peer group a development plan for improving their skill levels and knowledge of your industry and your organization's products and services. These plans may include in-house course material, outside seminars, classroom work and self-study.

One Acumen client hires professional actors to role-play client interactions and management reviews. Using other outside experts who specialize in communication, presentation, tactical field management and psychological assessment can all help strengthen your certification program. And like all long-term training initiatives, your program's content, maturity and acceptance will evolve over time.

Why now?

There's never been a better time to launch a certification program. In the past, companies faced immense costs for creating, delivering, managing and updating organization-wide certification programs. Today, thanks to online training tools, laptop computers, internet and intranet access and a variety of monitoring and assessment tools, are making such programs much more affordable. Using online training helps reduce travel costs as well.

With the advent of e-business, multi-channel issues and international competition, businesses need cost-effective delivery now more than ever. The increase in offerings and similarities between the offerings in many product and service categories brings us back to the real difference in most organizations -- our people. We must commit to making them our true company differentiators. Creating and maintaining a sales-certification program offers an excellent way to achieve that goal.

30 | CUSTOMIZING COMPENSATION

Here's how to create a compensation system that works for your sales team — and helps meet your company's goals.

When it comes to how businesses pay their salespeople, there's no one-size-fits-all approach. After all, each company has its own business model, margins and mix of products and services. Some pay commissions based on sales, while others only pay on margin; still others blend both with incentives and special bonus plans.

No matter which approach you use, success depends on awareness. Your sales management team must understand your company's overall goals, and then structure compensation to align with them. In short, sales compensation should be not just a tactical focus for your organization, but a strategic one as well.

Sizing It Up

Compensation plans shouldn't be developed in a vacuum. You and your sales leaders need a solid grasp of your overall industry and your organization's place in it. You'll need to factor in variables such as new product or service launches and major promotions, and you'll need to consider your personnel structure, too. You should also address these questions:

- Is your company a start-up or an established business?

- Are your sales goals orders, bookings or invoices based?

- How long are your delivery cycles?

- What are your objectives: to secure new clients, increase average order size, reduce selling expenses?

- Do you want to open new geographic or vertical markets, focus on the profitable aspects of your business or increase certain activities, such as cold calling?

Each answer will help them design a compensation plan tailored to your company's specific requirements.

Finally, take a hard look at your sales organization. Take the time to set goals and analyze gaps. For instance, do you need to attract new representatives to make C-level sales calls? Do you want to retain employees to build a long-term, client-based sales team, or is rapid turnover acceptable because it provides new blood? Such considerations also play into compensation planning.

Understanding Cost of Sales (CoS)

Of course, you can reduce selling costs and enhance profits by capping sales compensation, but in the long run you get what you pay for. If you hire good salespeople and compensate them poorly, expect high turnover, which comes with its own costs. Rewarding performance will help you to attract and retain keep the best people.

Calculating the cost of sales (CoS) is an important part of planning a compensation package. For a quick CoS ratio, simply take an individual's salary plus commissions earned at 100 percent of quota and potential bonus opportunities, then divide by that person's revenues to obtain the percentage. For example, if a salesperson earns $150,000 in total compensation and sells $1.5 million of products and services, his CoS is 10 percent. A more sophisticated approach adds in marketing expenses, corporate overhead, direct expenses paid to the salesperson and sales- support costs.

Once you have determined an acceptable CoS range, you can fine-tune the commission plan.

Examining the Options

Compensation plans vary widely, but all should include "accelerators"--that is, increased commission rates for employees who achieve target sales levels. Following are a few common examples of different plan structures:

- **Profit-Based:** Commission rates change as margin levels increase. These plans are generally based on invoice, product or monthly averages of margin generation.

- **Revenue/Quota:** Compensation is based on sheer volume achieved over the previous sales period or on a percentage of a quota achievement.

- **Balanced:** Compensation is based on margin, revenue and a third component, such as quota attainment.

- **Team:** Bonuses go to all team members when quarter-to-date (QTD) sales goals are achieved.

Let's examine which types of plans work best in which scenarios. If your company has high revenue-growth objectives in a boom market with little competition, use a plan with aggressive accelerators. Another option involves offering higher base salaries and lower commissions. An advantage to this approach: You may not need reps with top-notch sales skills because, in this case, they're primarily order-takers.

The situation changes in a slower-growing market with many competitors. Here, you might adopt a "protect-and-grow" revenue objective to play defense against rivals, while using a margin-based plan to upgrade accounts. The idea is to gear compensation to account for growth while providing bonuses for new accounts.

If your company's goal is to grow revenue and focus on new account conversion programs, choose a plan focused on the percentage of sales growth quarter over quarter or annually over named accounts. Certainly, using a quota-based compensation plan can achieve this objective, too. This scenario requires strong sales compensation with quarterly bonus emphasis on revenue gains from new business.

Special Circumstances

Following are a few other considerations that may come into play as you customize your compensation plan.

- **In existing markets:** For new organizations focused on expanding in existing markets, compensation plans will differ dramatically from those of established companies in the same industry. A mature, market-dominant company that receives a large percentage of its revenues from a small, loyal customer base can offer lower commissions and, perhaps, lower overall salaries. But a newcomer to an existing market probably needs to offer higher compensation to attract top-performing salespeople who can build a strong customer base.

- **In new markets:** New organizations in new markets need compensation plans reflecting the volatile environment, usually with higher-than-average base pay.

- **In transitions and turnarounds:** Companies in transition or undergoing a turnaround typically experience a higher CoS ratio. They may be best served by flexible plans incorporating morale- and team-building components, as well as six month compensation plans.

- **In high-growth environments:** Organizations positioned for high growth should develop plans covering just six-month periods. The shorter time frame will let management test theories and change direction while allowing the sales team to adjust accordingly.

Clearly, creating an effective sales compensation plan is hard work. But it's also clear that the effort typically pays off in both improved sales performance and achievement of your corporate goals.

For more detailed information regarding developing sales compensation review *The Sales Management Guru's Guide To: Developing Sales Compensations Work* at www.AcumenManagement.com

PART IV:
CULTURE

31 | CREATING YOUR TEAM & YOUR CULTURE

Building a great sales organization involves more than just bringing the right people on board. It requires providing the right opportunities and creating the right culture.

Recently, in speaking to two prospective clients, I heard the same complaint that I hear over and over from sales executives: "My turnover rate is huge."

They're not alone in their concerns. Consider these facts:

- In one Manpower Inc. survey of nearly 33,000 employers worldwide, U.S. and Canadian respondents both ranked "sales representative" as the job they were having most trouble filling.

- Nearly 25 percent of the nearly 2,200 sales executives surveyed in another major study reported that turnover had increased during the previous year.

Hiring the right talent is critical in building successful sales teams. Studies show that, if you bring in the wrong salesperson, you lose up to four times the cost of that person's annual salary and benefits in missed opportunities, management time, fee's and other factors. (If you're experiencing turnover, you may find Acumen's *Sales Manager Guru's Guide*

To: Hiring High-Performance Sales Teams a valuable resource at www.AcumenManagement.com)

Building Your Team: Beyond Hiring

However, hiring is just one part of the equation. It's also important to develop and retain your salespeople. Here are a few suggestions for achieving those goals:

- **Buff up the "B" team.** Obviously, you have a limited number of "A-level" salespeople. It makes sense to invest some effort in grooming the B-level team members who seem most likely to be able to move up to the top tier.

  If you're recruiting regularly, you'll have a constant pipeline of top talent available to keep enhancing the quality of your team. Conducting interviews regularly will improve your ability to identify both the winners and the runners-up — that is, the B-team players with strong potential.

  Don't waste time on salespeople who are C-level or below. Many sales managers spend too much valuable time attempting to save poor performers or trying to make their money back on their hiring mistakes. Instead, focus on providing B-level players with the management, coaching and training they need to advance.

- **Emphasize education.** Design a comprehensive orientation and training program to ensure that new hires hit the ground running--and that they keep moving forward.

  We typically advise our clients to establish a three-week on-boarding plan for new hires. That effort typically includes having new employees do everything from reading past proposals to learning to use the customer relationship management (CRM) system and other technologies to making presentations to multiple people, including the president. Managers or assisting salespeople should sign off on each item on each employee's new hire plan.

The plan should also include a 90-day list of planned objectives. While those objectives will be unique for each organization, they might include pipeline values, revenue goals, sales calls goals and proposals delivered. Having predefined objectives allows all involved to know whether each new hire is on track or requires some additional education.

- **Create a sales-oriented culture.** From conducting numerous exit interviews, we've found that many top salespeople leave their jobs not because they're dissatisfied with compensation, but because they're frustrated by sales management. Typically, that frustration stems from a culture that blocks sales success via lack of support, poorly designed sales processes and inefficient internal policies that make it difficult to add new clients, generate proposals, process orders or even calculate commissions. Some organizations call this as "sales prevention."

  Recognizing success goes a long way in building a strong sales culture. Offering contests, awards and yearly incentive trips--and maintaining a fun environment—are all important ways to provide that acknowledge.

Sales leaders serious about improving performance should work hard to implement all three suggestions, helping B-level players move up while developing training programs and a culture that encourages and reward success.

Building Your Team: Working with Company Leadership

Another critical step in building that culture is making sure that your company's leadership views sales development as a top priority.

That's not necessarily a given. Many companies' management teams view their sales divisions as cost centers. In reality, those divisions are profit centers. For that reason, executives should be doing everything possible to help their salespeople execute brilliantly. Again, companies serious about gaining competitive advantage should emphasize developing, mentoring and coaching their sales teams in the same way that they focus on building certification levels for their delivery teams.

Executives from smaller companies often tell us that, unlike their counterparts at larger enterprises, they don't have the resources to undertake professional-level development projects. (My typical response is: "That's why you're still a small company.") In reality, though, effective sales training and retention efforts are especially critical for small businesses. Cash flow and decreased sales can have a much bigger impact on monthly profitability for small businesses than for large companies, which can usually better weather a few bumps.

The takeaway: Building a strong sales organization requires developing programs dedicated to each salesperson's short-term success and long-term growth — and it requires doing so in a positive culture that rewards achievement. Such efforts will help all team members reach their potential and go a long way toward keeping them on board.

32 | BUILDING BELIEF FOR SALES SUCCESS

Company histories, client testimonials and entertaining sales meetings can help reinforce your team's sense of mission.

Are your sales inconsistent? Are you losing more opportunities than ever before? Does your sales team seem weak compared to those of your competitors?

Any number of reasons—from rapid growth to hiring mistakes—could be responsible for a "yes" answer to any of those questions. But in working with our clients, we at Acumen often find that the underlying problem is actually an emotional one: lack of passion. In other words, individual team members or the entire sales organization—or both—simply don't have the combination of enthusiasm and belief that's essential for success.

Salespeople must be emotionally invested in their work with a burning desire to achieve. They must also believe that the company they represent is the best and the solutions or services they sell are of the highest quality. That belief must be genuine. It's not just a marketing message, and it's not something that they can fake. Unfortunately, however, most sales organizations spend little or no time on belief-building activities.

Igniting the Spark

Our experience shows that the most successful sales organizations regularly undertake efforts to fuel team members' faith in what they're selling. Following are a few examples of belief-building initiatives that you might wish to try:

- **Storytelling:** People from different cultures and generations pass along stories about their ancestries, traditions and lore. Companies need to take a similar approach to capturing and preserving their histories. To do so, write down customer success stories when they occur. Assemble detailed descriptions of your company's role in helping customers implement new technologies, launch new projects or salvage existing ones. Then share these stories at sales meetings and other employee events. You can also use the best stories to recruit top performers and help orient new employees.

  Many of your company's stories could end up as case studies. But in terms of building belief, the stories' primary purpose is teaching employees about your organization's early years, solidifying their understanding of your company's philosophy and traditions.

- **Monthly meetings:** When a company starts up, its first employees typically feel that they share a mission. Everyone knows everything that's happening and what's needed to succeed. But when the staff grows beyond about 15 people, that sense of mission, as well as clearly defined expectations and common beliefs, can be difficult to maintain.

  We believe that monthly employee meetings are crucial for keeping everyone engaged and informed. (Larger organizations and those with remote offices may want to opt for quarterly day-long events instead.) Such gatherings give company leaders a chance to remind your staff about your business philosophies, plans and expectations. You can also use them to recognize outstanding employees, perhaps honoring a Most Valuable Player chosen by the team at each session.

Be sure to make these meetings fun as well. Consider sponsoring games or offering door prizes. One company meeting that I attended featured a surprise visit from an Elvis impersonator who sang several songs.

- **Customer visits:** Each quarter, have your entire sales team visit a one of your customer's companies that relies on your solutions and services. Ask the customer's executives to describe the impact that your company has had on their competitive position or to review the savings they've gained from what you've sold them.

  You might also invite customers to share their experiences at some of your monthly company meetings. There is nothing better for a salesperson than to hear a customer talk about the success they have had with your products/ service.

- **Reference letters:** Ask your customers for testimonials. While such letters are highly useful as tools for future sales presentations, they're also valuable for building belief in-house. Frame the letters and display them in your lobby or sales presentation area. (Guru Hint: Have all new employees read these letters as part of their orientation process. Doing so will help with both with building belief and pride in your firm.)

- **New-hire orientation:** If possible, arrange for all new employees to have lunch meetings with various management-team members. That provides an opportunity for your company's leaders to discuss their approach and demonstration their commitment to your organization's core values.

In our business, it's all too easy to get bogged down with lost sales, missed project dates and other problems. Regularly reinforcing the positives goes a long way toward keeping everyone's belief and passion strong and moving in the right direction.

33 | NICE GUYS CAN FINISH FIRST

When sales are flagging, you may feel compelled to bear down harder than ever on your salespeople. But there are better ways to get results.

Alec Baldwin's character, Blake, from the 1992 movie "Glengarry Glen Ross," isn't the sales manager most of us would like to work for or want to be.

But when you're facing the end of a brutal quarter or a rough year, the temptation to strike fear into the hearts of your salespeople can become overpowering. In my experience, however, when it's time to rewire a sales team for the balance of the year and prepare them for the next 12 months, you can find more productive ways than creating the poisonously competitive atmosphere fomented by Blake's "motivational" speech. Following are a few pointers for getting the job done.

Keep in mind that:

1. **As a manager, you should show how much you care.**

   I once had a sales manager sit down with me to talk about what I wanted to get out of the job in the following two to three years. The discussion was very helpful, and it left me feeling that he cared about me as a person, not just as an employee. If you understand the person, you can align the person's motivations to your company goals.

Long term, the most important motivations are always self-generated. When you help employees learn to be more successful at sales, they'll be more motivated. Success and motivation create a psychological feedback system.

Nothing can motivate a salesperson more than knowing the manager has his or her back and is interested in feedback on important issues such as goals, incentives and understanding how the company is working.

2. **Sales motivation is closely related to sales confidence.**

    Especially in challenging times, leaders need to focus on building their representatives' self-confidence. Many salespeople aren't used to not selling, so they begin to question themselves.

    Stress levels often increase during tough times, and increased stress levels can impair salesperson's ability to create trust and confidence with prospective client. To increase and maintain employee self-confidence, sales leaders should beef up training, role-playing and in-the-field coaching -- all with a positive approach and combined with honest praise.

3. **Fun is still an important motivator even in serious business situations.**

    The best annual sales-achievement contests involve an incentive trip. This isn't an expense; instead, it should be paid for in incremental sales dollars. I recommend always having a quarterly sales game in place to drive activity, sales or other corporate objectives. The key is giving everyone the opportunity to win — and keeping things fun.

4. **Public recognition is another great practice for motivating your sales staff.**

   Giving recognition to salespeople in front of their peers -- and in front of management -- can be a huge motivating force. Your monthly company meeting can be a good time to recognize all orders, honor top-producing salespeople and acknowledge other achievements. Find something so that you can praise everyone on your team. You might also mail letters to the homes of your top-achieving salespeople, congratulating them on their performance.

5. **Team incentives are another option.**

   I like to recommend that a portion of your compensation plan includes a team bonus. If everyone on the team hits 100 percent of your company's quota, everyone wins. This bonus value -- say, $5,000 — can be divided among sales-team members based on their individual contributions towards achieving the goal. I also recommend providing bonuses to your marketing person and pre-sales support person if the team hits its numbers.

   Why does all this matter? Because in tough times, it's especially important to keep everyone working together to achieve their mutual goals. A team that works cooperatively develops dependence and camaraderie.

   These days, motivation is more critical than ever. Investing in your people is equally important, and as a strategic sales leader, making sure you are personally focused on your people will make the difference. Beyond that, motivating your team members with support, rewards and recognition will work far better in the long run than trying to manage them with negativity and fear.

34 | SALES CONTESTS: PLAYING TO WIN

Here are the goals and ideas for growing sales organically through contests — and having some fun in the process.

Sales contests are important ingredients for exceeding your revenue targets, building high-performing sales teams and even creating the right organizational culture — one that's both sales-driven and fun.

Different types of contests will help you achieve different goals. Some should be held annually to address sales objectives, company business strategies and potential seasonal fluctuations. Others can be scheduled as needed to help launch new products or services, promote new releases or upgrades or tie into your vendors' larger campaigns. Still others can consist of short-term incentive games designed to motivate sales personnel to accomplish specific objectives by a specific deadline.

A Contest Sampler

Following are a few typical goals, along with ideas for contests that may help achieve them:

- **Increasing sales volume.** Consider adding a cash bounty for each additional new product, new customer, or revenue sold beyond a certain target value. Set a quarter-to-date objective above your sales goal; that way, everyone on the team can win.

- **Improving customer service.** Periodically survey your entire customer base. If satisfaction reaches a certain goal — for instance, when 95 percent of your clients say they're "highly satisfied" — and if your company is profitable, everyone gets a cash bonus. Keep a visible scorecard of your goals and results so that everyone maintains a constant awareness of your objectives.

- **Acquiring new clients.** To boost the number of net new clients you add each quarter, consider creating a "bounty bonus" plan. For example, salespeople could earn a bounty bonus — either in cash or in points that can be redeemed for rewards — for each new client or each competitive replacement of a specific vendor's customer. In addition, you could offer bounty bonuses for salespeople who exceed their quarterly or annual quotas for new accounts or net new revenues. You might even create and post "Most Wanted" posters with the bounties prominently displayed to help keep salespeople focused on contest objectives.

- **Overcoming seasonal slumps.** If your sales typically slow down over the summer, try launching a prospecting activity contest in March, April and May. For instance, award sales team members points for each new face-to-face call or sales demonstrations that they make during those months, with accumulated points eventually eligible for prizes. Such an effort can go a long way toward increasing the number of opportunities in the pipeline from June through August.

Contest Considerations

Following are some issues to consider and questions to answer as you plan sales contests:

- **Determine what you want the contest to accomplish.** Will it add incremental new business levels or simply shift future orders to a nearer term?

- **Set the ground rules.** Are all sales executives on an equal basis for the contest? Can everyone win-or just certain team members? Be sure to put the rules in writing, making provisions for those and other situations that could arise.

- **Make the contest length the same as the sales cycle.** Depending upon your sales cycle, a 30-day sales contest may not be effective because, of course, all prospects are already in the pipeline, ready to close.

- **Set specific goals that can be measured weekly or monthly.** Create a visible tracking tool to show the results. Share them with your salespeople and your management team.

- **Incorporate an exciting theme.** If your top prize is a dream vacation, post pictures of the destination and build your annual sales slogan or motto around the goal of winning that trip. As the sales leader, you must get your team fired up for the contest.

- **Consider making rewards gifts, rather than cash.** Salespeople may want you to "show them the money," but, in truth, cash bonuses are typically wasted and soon forgotten. Instead, try awarding something tangible, whether it's a laser pointer, a gift certificate to a local clothing store or an expenses-paid weekend getaway.

- **Boost team members' motivation by getting their families involved.** For long-term games involving significant gifts or major trips, send rules and teaser gifts to salespeople's homes after announcing the contest at work. Send congratulatory letters to winners' homes as well.

- **Never run contests to the last day of the month or sales period.** Halting them five days before the end of the month allows time for making your month's objectives. If all goes well, you'll exceed your targets — with nearly a week to spare.

35 | COMPETITION & COLLABORATION

The best salespeople don't just try to outsell their rivals—they try to build long-term customer relationships as well. Here's how to help your team strike the right balance.

In today's complex, overheated sales environment, many opportunities involve at least two competitors. At the same time, customers increasingly expect salespeople to serve as trusted business advisors. That means that sales teams must work at building solid relationships as well as winning sales.

Top sales performers have always been competitive. Beyond that, the best salespeople I know possess a few basic winning traits. They're creative and energetic. They're able to out-strategize their rivals. And they're able to overcome objections and generate the emotion that turns a prospect into a client.

In addition, these same top performers are typically collaborative as well. They focus on more than just making the immediate sale. They try hard to genuinely understand each prospect and develop proposals offering clear long-time value. They work at building long-term partnerships with their customers.

Two Steps to Achieving the Right Balance

So how do you make sure that your own sales team reflects the optimal combination of competition and collaboration? Just follow this two-step process.

1. **Know your team and your markets.** Understand that different vertical markets and types of organizations may require different sales approaches—and different team members may be better at providing them. For example, if one salesperson excels at selling into a nonprofit organization made up of multiple decision-makers who must reach a consensus, it's unlikely that that same person will do well at selling into a highly entrepreneurial small or midsize company.

   Identifying your markets and your customers' buying patterns will help you determine your ideal ratio of competitiveness to collaboration.

   Hint: One place to start: Interview at least 10 existing clients about the characteristics they prefer in their sales reps. Ask them for adjectives that describe an ideal salesperson and what they like in how a salesperson works with them. This exercise will help you identify the common characteristics you are looking for during the interview process.

2. **Set your own ideal standards for balance.** Acumen recommends using an online assessment tool that allows you to establish the styles, skills and characteristics -- including competitiveness, ethics and collaborative ability -- that you most want in your salespeople. You can then use these tools to interview candidates to see how well they match those requirements.

   As an aside: Remember that such assessment tools are just one option for hiring and the results generated shouldn't, by themselves, be viewed as automatic pass/fail decisions. (Interested in learning about tools from several vendors? E-mail me at ken@acumenmgmt.com for a list.)

Bottom line: Prospects need help in making decisions. A salesperson's collaborative side helps prospects see why particular options are in their best interests, while the competitive side provides the mental toughness to bring the discussion to a positive close. For that reason, the final step for establishing the right balance is to remind all team members to continue developing both abilities.

36 | THE SELF-MANAGED SALES TEAM

Requiring salespeople to create personal "road maps" for success can help them all become self-starters — and put your entire organization on track for success.

It's the dream of just about every leader at just about every company: "We'll hire the best salespeople and let them go sell so that we can focus on running the business. After all, they should know what to do."

As a result, many companies fall into the same trap: They hire those salespeople, turn their own attention to other aspects of the business and then check in months later to find a disturbing lack of results.

The good news: It's possible to turn that dream of a self-managed, high-performance sales team into reality. But doing so requires a well-coordinated approach. And success depends upon clearly defining expectations and providing salespeople with the tools they need to reach their goals.

Build a Strong Foundation

Any effective self-management initiative will be based on these three critical assumptions:

1. **Sales leaders must provide sales teams with guidance.** Assuming that salespeople can manage themselves with no direction will lead to failure. A completely hands-off approach will result in missed opportunities, untapped markets, wasted sales and marketing budgets and cash-flow problems.

2. **Sales leaders must set expectations for all involved.** Failing to set clear expectations will create frustration for everyone. Managers and salespeople must agree upon targets for monthly and quarterly activity levels and well-defined margin/revenue goals.

3. **Sales leaders must verify the initiative's results.** Pledging to "inspect what you expect" is critical for self-management success. This means verifying that all salespeople understand your offerings, represent your organization professionally and sell effectively. When combined with a couple of simple tools, this mindset will help ensure that your sales team is working as well as possible.

A Step-by-Step Plan

Begin by having salespeople create individual, six-month business plans describing their goals, training needs, quotas and forecasts as defined by specific clients and products. These personal plans should also include sales-activity goals and coordinating local marketing activities with any customer marketing programs. Ultimately, the plans create road maps that all salespeople — and sales management — can review regularly to gauge their progress.

Next, have each salesperson prepare a quarterly account-planning document listing up to five specific steps or methods for opening or further penetrating specific accounts. This tool allows salespeople to define the important aspects of each account, including key contacts, information about the competition and details on past successes. With that information, they can develop account strategies, including specific sales tactics to be executed during the time covered by the plan. Each tactic must have an agreed to action and a planned completion date associated with it. Both the salesperson business plan and account plan allow for a proactive approach to sales management.

These tools allow managers to monitor both current and past performance, measuring results against each person's desired objectives, then providing coaching as needed. They can also help ensure that a sales organization is consistently building pipeline values that provide enough prospect opportunity to exceed individual quotas or personal goals. Everyone understands what's supposed to happen; everyone can monitor how well current activity measures up to planned approaches and results.

Because salespeople have developed the tools themselves, they will "own" their activities and are more likely to work steadily toward achieving their goals. At that point, they become self-managed.

Finally, salespeople should meet quarterly with the company's key management-team members, including the CFO and vice presidents of marketing and production, to review the new plans and objectives. Team members should also share their individual business and account plans with each other, on a quarterly basis. This exercise not only documents commitment to the team, but also creates the potential for collaboration — and even a little peer pressure.

The true power of these personalized plans becomes evident when they're measured against actual performance. When salespeople face quarterly reviews in which they must discuss how successfully they met their targets and then recommit to their new plans, they truly "get it." They understand what it takes to achieve their goals and how specific planning leads to improved performance. As you lead them through this process, you'll see self-management take hold, moving from concept to practice -- and from dream to reality.

37 | THE POWER OF 'NET NEW'

Following are some considerations and action items designed to help you capture and build relationships with 'net new' clients.

Lately, I've been reflecting on trends I've noticed over the past few years during my work helping many different companies build predictable revenue. One major trend that I observed: the growing emphasis on adding net new clients.

We've found that, over a three-year period, clients who increase their focus on net new clients and use careful execution to obtain them experience greater percentages of revenue growth than those who don't.

Before beginning this discussion, let me define a "net new" client. The term can refer to a prospect that your company has never previously sold products or services, or to one that you haven't in engaged with in a significant amount of time — say, the past five years.

So what are some factors companies can consider and actions they can take to achieve to land those net new clients — and achieve that revenue growth?

From a leadership perspective, the first action item should be setting the vision or goal, and then determining whether the entire management committee is committed to achieving that vision or goal. If the answer is yes, it's time to set the first metric: a specific number of net new clients to be sold per quarter. Depending upon the size of your organization, you may elect to determine metrics for net new revenue and net new clients per quarter by practice or department.

The second action item entails creating a marketing plan to assist in attracting net new prospects. Expect to spend additional marketing dollars rather than simply reaching out to your existing customer base once or twice. We typically recommend that you "touch" each prospect eight to 12 times by e-mail, direct mail, phone calls and any other methods. In fact, the secret to a highly successful campaign is touching various job titles at each prospective organization, such as the president, the CFO and the vice presidents of sales, marketing, human resources, manufacturing and so on. Guru Hint: Make sure that your marketing messages are unique and specific to the person who holds each job title.

The third action item is reviewing your sales-compensation plans or holding sales contests to build awareness of and excitement around management's interest in this objective. For compensation plans, we often create an additional percentage or dollar bonus on all net new clients sold *if* sales or revenues are greater than a certain dollar figure. These may be based on monthly or quarterly objectives. In some cases, we set up a sales contest based on convincing customers to replace a competitor's product or service with our client's product or services. Marketing should be aligned with this campaign as well, and "wanted" posters with the bonus amounts prominently featured can be displayed in the sales team's work area.

The fourth action item in your game plan is making sure that top management consistently reinforces its vision for the entire company as well as for the sales team, at monthly company meetings, sales meetings and in written communications, where appropriate.

Finally, it's important to create a dashboard or scorecard. This is the measurement tool that shows existing and past performance against the stated objective both by company and by individual salesperson. From a current status perspective, sales leaders would want to track:

- Number of net new calls per week/month
- Number of net new proposals per month
- Number of net new opportunities in the pipeline
- Dollar value of all net new opportunities in the pipeline
- Number of net new opportunities sold, quarter to date (QTD) and year to date (YTD)
- Dollar value of net new opportunities sold QTD and YTD

The classic saying "What gets measured gets managed" certainly applies here. You'll achieve the desired results if you pay attention to objectives, execution and the activities of both sales and marketing. We also like to recommend that you graph these numbers mentioned above to provide a trend analysis. Doing so will help you link the marketing and sales activities to results and will also help salespeople better understand the correlation between goals, actions and results.

Every month, company leadership and sales management should both ask the same questions: Are we on target? If not, why not? How are we going to fix the problem? Once you capture your net new clients, you have a new goal: earning a greater portion of their "wallet share." The second, third and fourth sales will be increasingly easier and should earn higher levels of profitability. That allows you start recording a new metric: account penetration ratio. This number reflects the annual increase in dollars spent with your firm by each client.

38 | WHAT CAN I DO TODAY TO SELL SOMETHING?

At Acumen, we like to see this this question posted in all our clients' work areas. It's a reminder that can reap significant results.

In challenging times, and even in good ones, it's essential to keep everyone in your organization focused on the business's ultimate objectives, adding new clients and additional revenues. Distractions can waste valuable time and result in lost opportunities. Serving existing clients is, of course, important — but adding "wallet share" or increasing client penetration ratios is just as critical.

One of our own sales-management mottos is: Make sure that everyone understands the difference between *direction* and *motion*. In other words: Are you moving forward with a clear destination in mind? Or are you simply staying busy, doing things that need to be done — but that don't necessarily drive sales and profits?

One way to underscore that difference between motion and direction is requiring every salesperson to create a short-term execution plan that's well-defined and well-measured and that emphasizes the importance of constantly moving toward sales. We recommend that each week, each salesperson reviews the next two sales actions that he or she plans to take with each prospect over the next 60 days.

You'll also help improve sales representatives' focus if, during a sales meeting, you ask them to describe their personal prospecting plans for the next 30 days. Some plans may demonstrate creativity while others may be disappointing, but holding this exercise during team meetings can help people share ideas and energize each other.

Another method for providing a fast injection of sales revenue is developing an "attack plan" for existing clients. Following are instructions for doing that:

1. **Analyze your client base.** Determine what products and services you've sold to each client. Next, determine whether or how you might upgrade those solutions. Next, figure out what products and services you haven't sold them and how you will approach each one to introduce new solutions. Guru tip: Think about whether you or another salesperson has sold one of those products or services to another client. How can you use your success to introduce those solutions to other clients?

2. **Make a plan.** Create a six-week plan for contacting every client with specific marketing and sales plans. Include at least one action that management and salespeople should take each week. Build in a mechanism for making sure that you've reached each client during that period. Make sure you have built in a tracking tool to ensure that your sales teams are executing on the plan, making contact with each client.

3. **Consider other approaches.** You might offer clients a 90-day trial on a special package of products or services. Or you could hold a client-appreciation event, or, over a two-week period, thank each client with a special offer. Even if clients aren't ready to upgrade or invest in new solutions right now, you could ask them to write refer-

ence letters that you can include in your sales materials to drive other sales. Guru tip: Posting these endorsements in your lobby can also send a powerful message for visiting prospects and both existing and new employees.

4. **Build a referral offer.** For each sales call, set a goal of requesting at least one new prospect's name from the client. That simple step can generate additional sales activity and potentially result in net new clients. In addition, encourage salespeople to ask each client—in every conversation—to recommend or refer other people they might contact. We suggest posting a reminder about this step in each salesperson's work area.

5. **Remember the most important question.** Keep asking your sales team—and yourself—what else can we do to sell something today? Other questions to consider: Does each salesperson know when each prospective client wants to be fully utilizing your solutions? Do you have your closing strategy in place? For more, visit the Guru's Web site (www.acumenmanagement.com) and blog (www.YourSalesManagementGuru.com).

39 | THE NEXT EIGHTEEN MONTHS

Adopt the Acumen Philosophy to position your company for growth in the next year-plus.

During the best *and* the worst of times, the companies that typically stand out are those that demonstrate appreciation for the importance of execution and measurement. "Core competencies" or "best practices" seem to be the best descriptions for these focus points.

Over the past 20 years, we at Acumen Management have observed that the most successful companies are those focused on the following points of excellence:

- Management decisions
- People and culture
- Activity levels
- Customer results
- Company results

In the business world, management has traditionally analyzed financial statements, re-engineered system and manufacturing processes, and reviewed marketing effectiveness. CEOs have strengthened balance sheets with better asset management, reduced inventory and cost levels with "just-in-time" methodology, and increased direct-mail and advertising effectiveness with testing and reporting methods. But as we've mentioned elsewhere in this book, the focus has shifted to the last bastion of corporate analysis: the sales organization.

Today's corporate boards are scrutinizing strategic sales management, sales productivity, the analysis of pipeline and forecasting accuracy, dollar values, cost of sales, market share, sales process, lifetime values and salesperson effectiveness. All organizations are now under pressure to create consistently profitable sales-distribution organizations.

In response to this emphasis on strategic sales management, we've developed "the Acumen Philosophy," a list of traits and values that characterize successful companies. We believe that:

- Business development effectiveness is essential.
- Business strategies come first.
- The best practices are consistent from industry to industry.
- Sales must be a corporate priority.
- Structured process is critical for to success.
- Teamwork prevails.
- Training and recruitment are sales-organization priorities.
- Compensation is linked to corporate objectives.
- Corporate image and branding is important.
- Corporate culture is deep and consistent.

If companies adhere to these values but aren't functioning or executing effectively, it's typically because they lack strategic and tactical sales plans. Such plans should include:

- An amalgamation of the organization's goals
- Individual salespeople's goals
- Coordination of marketing and sales tactics
- A common set of measurement factors ensuring that all parties are focused on the right activities for generating success

We believe that when companies focus on aligning employees' souls with the corporation's goals, success naturally follows. This psychological balance with the corporate focus brings together the essential elements necessary for sales teams to execute at high levels. This type of management structure aids everyone, so it's typically readily accepted by sales teams.

Creating the Right Management Structure

First, focus on creating individual salesperson business plans that define and bring together each salesperson's goals with the organization's goals and that also coordinate activity with planned marketing programs. These plans should integrate territory plans and/or named account plans for specific time periods.

An effective planning tool asks the salesperson to identify:

- Personal objectives or goals
- Personal and professional developmental goals
- Income goals
- Activity goals (from above)
- Territory analysis

- Forecasted revenues by account
- Total forecasted revenues for the period
- Quota-attainment goals
- Monthly marketing plans for six months
- Specific account strategies and planned tactics

Using a sales management-planning tool dramatically shifts the sales manager's focus from the past to the future. While most CRM or manual sales-management systems can enhance a sales organization's effectiveness, they generally measure past activities and current sales funnel values. While that's important information for sales teams to know, such systems fall short by providing a rearview-mirror methodology to managing. The sales manager is simply reacting to what has already happened.

One new technology trend involves sales-management software, which has quickly become more important than CRM software. That's not surprising considering that, by some reports, CRM has experienced a 66 percent implementation-failure rate.

In addition, sales managers and salespeople often have no forward-looking plans or focus about what they should be achieving in their territories or accounts. A properly designed sales-management planning tool changes that situation. With such tools, the sales manager can monitor expected performance, serve as a coach or mentor, provide a viewpoint of past performance and measure results against the salesperson's desired objectives. In addition, a forward- looking individual marketing plan can help both the salesperson and sales manager begin look far enough ahead to build pipeline values that will provide enough prospect opportunity to exceed individual quotas or personal goals.

As with any new organizational change, the rollout must be carefully planned. We suggest the following steps:

1. Each business-planning tool must be carefully explained to salespeople.

2. Salespeople should attend group meetings with their colleagues and management-team members such as the CFO and the vice presidents of marketing and production.

3. Salespeople should present business plans and account plans to their peer groups and management teams.

4. Salespeople must submit drafts to their managers for review and edit before group meetings.

This approach of real value is realized when your salespeople measure their plans against their actual performance. That's the point when salespeople truly "get it." They recognize what it takes to achieve their personal and professional goals, and they see how creating better planning impacts their performance — and the company's as well.

These tools are excellent for new salespeople taking over existing territories. They also help sales managers provide better, more accurate forecasts to corporate management. Acument's *"Online Interactive Sales Managers' Tool Kit"* offers both account and salesperson business planning tools.

The next requirement for effective sales management planning is constant measurement. Your company must identify common success metrics for your sales team. To do this, determine at least four key indicators for measuring success for all salespeople with common responsibilities. Monthly metrics might include, by salesperson:

• Ratio of forecasted revenue ratio to actual monthly revenue

- Number of proposals or quotes generated
- Number of new accounts added to the pipeline
- Number of company visits

For new salespeople, one indicator could be the time it takes for them to become productive — 30 days, 60 days or 90 days. If it takes the salesperson substantially longer than expected to achieve productive revenue, you may need to consider retraining that person — or possibly even letting him or her go.

Increasing levels of activity or numbers of prospects doesn't necessarily mean increasing sales, so ratios can provide important measurements. Sales managers must develop each salesperson's closing ratios--that is, how many prospects it takes to attain the monthly quota or your company's revenue expectations and measuring the number of proposals delivered as opposed to the number of orders received. Analyze each salesperson's ratios, and then roll them all into a combined ratio for the entire sales team.

It's important to know the specific ratio of the revenue forecast to the percentage of actual revenue achieved. Graph this forecast-to-actual-performance ratio monthly for each salesperson and for the entire team. Build pride in forecast accuracy and this measurement will help you coach on qualification requirements.

Action item: Find your four (or more) leading indicators, set the standards and track them. Graphing them and letting the team see everyone's trends illustrates what it takes to succeed and, as a bonus, serves as a great coaching tool.

It's important for sales leaders to recognize that declining leading indicators foretell potential revenue downturns. But if you catch these trends early on, you can take steps to turn around declining revenues.

Using proper sales-management planning tools, measuring goals against actual performance and bringing salespeople into key review and planning processes will create the culture, commitment and focus characteristic of world-class sales teams.

PART V:

BONUS SPECIAL REPORT

The Job of Sales Management

Building Predictable Revenue

Bonus	THE JOB OF SALES
Special	MANAGEMENT
Report	A Prescriptive Approach
	to Defining Duties and
	Responsibilities

The ideal sales manager acts as a sales leader, a catalyst for change and continuous improvement, and a positive force within the larger organization. The best managers understand their priorities and their teams—and they have a vision for the future.

The report is designed to define key actions that the sales manager (SM) must take to be effective, then describe each action's purpose and explain its importance. Among the areas we'll cover are sales achievement, marketing plan development and execution, salesperson development, systematic management, recruitment and management communication. Note: The actions aren't listed in order of priority.

Sales Achievement

Purpose: Sales management's top objectives are driving sales, capturing new revenue and exceeding monthly sales and margin objectives. The following action list is designed to keep those objectives—also known as sales achievement— constantly in focus.

- **Action:** Undertake sales-strategy development with each salesperson on Monday morning and in a formal one-on-one meeting during the week.

  - This step helps ensure that each salesperson has effective strategies in place and is focused on the right opportunities (for additional assistance, see Acumen's tools at www.acumenmgmt.com/sales-manager.php).

- **Action:** Use strategic tools and questioning techniques to ensure that your team is going after qualified prospects and using valid strategies to reach them.

  - This step will also teach salespeople to use the right tool sets, think strategically and work smarter.

- **Action:** Attend key sales calls early in the sales process and help close sales opportunities.

  - By taking this action, you can better understand the opportunity and the people involved. Getting involved at the end of the sales process also helps strengthen relationships with prospects.

  - The SM's role is in these calls is important for establishing the company's credibility. You'll also learn to be a better coach.

- **Action:** Review pipeline analysis and qualification to ensure that adequate values exist.

  - The SM should always be looking 90 days beyond the current date to ensure that sales and marketing pipelines carry the opportunities needed to meet the organization's goals.

  - The SM should track both values and numbers of opportunities and should know the ratios between future pipeline values and future monthly quotas. It's important to undertake this exercise twice a month, and to launch new marketing campaigns as needed.

- **Action:** Document and post the top 10 largest sales opportunities in a highly visible location.

  - This action showcases large opportunities that can "make" the month as well as average opportunities that help move the team toward achieving quota.

  - Posting the top 10 opportunities helps keep the sale team focused. Failing to do so increases the likelihood of "out-of-sight, out-of-mind" syndrome, with opportunities buried inside the company's customer relationship management (CRM) system.

- **Action:** Keep the top sales opportunities -- by salesperson, by month -- constantly visible.

  - Keep in mind that visibility breeds focus. Have salespeople post reminders of those top opportunities in their personal workspaces.

  - As the SM, you should keep close tabs on pipeline values and specific accounts to make sure that each salesperson is keeping both top of mind. Encourage salespeople to bring the opportunity lists to the weekly Monday morning meeting.

- **Action:** Create a defined sales process. Ensure that the sales team understands and follows it.

  - This workflow is designed to keep salespeople working their opportunities in a consistent, proven format. It's important for the sales process to build trust and confidence—but it must also prove your value proposition.

  - The SM should design, document and manage the process to make sure sales actions are in alignment with the buyer's purchasing process.

- **Action:** Clearly monitor and track monthly objectives versus sales and revenues and metrics by salesperson.
  - This action helps you create the correct formulas for measuring the effectiveness of the organization's marketing, sales and sales activities. The goal is not only to track numbers, but also to work with individual salespeople on improving the results.
  - Because capabilities differ widely from salesperson to salesperson, it's important to personalize action plans. Creating a "dashboard" or scorecard helps document the correct level of activities for each salesperson.

Marketing Plan Development and Execution

Purpose: Creating an effective company marketing program requires both careful design and brilliant execution. Effective marketing will ensure creation of the correct number and value of opportunities along with long-term brand recognition.

- **Action:** Create key marketing messages and value propositions for the company.
  - This action is critical to ensure that everyone in the company can correctly transmit these messages.
  - The SM must focus on the value proposition is to ensure that it clearly describes what the company does, why its customers buy from it and how it differs from its competition.
- **Action:** Create a rolling six-month marketing calendar that incorporates all aspects of a go-to-market

campaign for touching key market segments.

- This action helps sales management to build an on-going level of lead generation and generate local, regional and/or national recognition.

- Be sure to include public-relations initiatives, networking events, monthly seminars, industry events and the like. The calendar includes events that the SM may or may not personally attend.

- **Action:** Develop an ongoing series of marketing events to drive lead generation by product, practice or service.

  - This action ensures that these practices are included in the marketing program.

  - The SM must focus on a balanced sales program to ensure there is effective use of all support teams and that sales are in alignment with corporate goals.

- **Action:** Develop an ongoing series of networking events to build market awareness.

  - This action, part of the overall marketing plan, is designed to ensure that all salespeople attend specific networking events.

  - The SM should be involved in networking, along with the salespeople and others in the organization. That helps ensure that the sales team is expanding the company's sphere of influence, understanding trends and seeking partners to leverage for additional sales opportunities.

- **Action:** Develop a public-relations program to build market awareness. Create a media outreach campaign, focusing on reaching key writers and editors who are cover the company's industry.

- This action, also part of the overall marketing plan, focuses on building long-term relationships with key media representatives.

- The SM should nurture these local and national PR campaigns to lower marketing costs and create a unique position of awareness in the community.

- **Action:** Within the defined sales process, create a methodology to prove the value proposition in conjunction with sales actions above.

  - The SM must build in actions or steps that allow prospects to see and feel why the company's messaging is real. That's important because many salespeople simply speak to the value proposition--but don't actually demonstrate it.

- **Action:** Create creative brochures, website pages and other sales information that represent your company's various offerings. Be sure that each of these collateral items is clear and focuses on your key messages.

  - This action ensures that the sales team has the appropriate "leave-behinds" and tools that describe the benefits your organization provides.

  - Use these materials to assist salespeople in selling the company and help prospective clients better understand your messaging. In many cases, those messages get diluted during the sales process. In addition, marketing needs the sales organization's front-line input.

- **Action:** Create a client-advisory council made up of five to seven clients. Meet with the council three times a year to gain insights into the market.

  - This step can help the SM better understand the market and build opportunities accordingly. Client-advisory council members can help the SM evaluate the quality of existing offerings and test out new ideas.

Salesperson Training and Development

Purpose: Actively focusing on salesperson development is essential for building a culture that breeds long-term sales success. Sales management must focus on training sales teams both in the office and in the field. A well-trained sales team is sharp, strong and confident, steadily increasing win rates. Following are examples of training actions:

- **Action:** Establish a new hire on-boarding process and closely track closely the new salesperson's development.
  - This action is critical for helping the new hire ramp up quickly, gaining the knowledge and skills needed to sell effectively.
  - By overseeing the quick-start program, the SM also sets initial performance expectations.
- **Action:** Create and publish a 90-day sales training program for the entire sales team. The program should covers sales skills, product and industry knowledge and company operations.
  - This action helps sales managers keep their teams sharp and updated. Tip: Assign your own salespeople to serve as trainers in these events.
  - Why 90 days? Because it helps the entire team move forward each quarter in terms of skills development. A 90-plan also allows enough time to thoroughly cover a wide variety of skills, making the longer-term approach better than weekly or 30-day sales training programs.

- **Action:** Bring in outside speakers, customers and training organizations to reinforce sales skills development and performance.

  - Introducing new voices can help reinforce existing sales policy while still introducing fresh ideas to your team.

  - Using professional sales educators as well as in-house training broadens skill levels and creates a common language for the sales team.

- **Action:** Create a salesperson development process and use it twice a year to review each person (for details on Acumen's Sales Certification Program, visit acumen-mgmt.com/certificates.phtml).

  - This plan helps individual team members grow professionally as they progress toward their goals.

  - Using the formal development review process helps sales managers evaluate and better communicate with salespeople while setting clearer expectations for all.

- **Action:** Coach and mentor each salesperson before and after sales calls to prospects, using Acumen's coaching tips.

  - This practice helps sales managers teach salespeople proper pre-call planning discipline and assists them with evaluating the effectiveness of their sales calls.

  - Make the following a routine question in all training and mentoring sessions: "If you had that call to do over again, what—if anything—would you do differently?" Coaching this way will help teach salespeople to coach themselves when the SM isn't with them on future sales calls.

- **Action**: Twice each year, have each salesperson read a high-quality book on sales, then discuss it with the SM and the rest of the team.

  - Incorporating reading into the sales training process helps leverage and reinforce training concepts.

  - During the reading period, assign each salesperson a certain number of book chapters to read each week. Schedule a time for salespeople to discuss what they've learned and how it applies to your company and your sales processes.

- **Action:** Make sales calls with sales-team members each month to monitor their performance.

  - This action helps you, as the SM, evaluate the team's development by "inspecting what you expect" from them in real-life situations. The goal: assessing whether individual salespeople are applying the right skills at the right time in the field.

- **Action:** Role-play during training sessions.

  - This step allows salespeople to practice their skills before going out to live customer meetings—and reassures the SM that team members know how to sell the company.

Systematic Management

Purpose: Taking a systematic approach to management allows the SM to operate easily and effectively operate in a high-pressure environment that's filled with distractions and requires multi-taking. Following are activities that support a systematic approach.

- **Action:** Use an agenda for your weekly sales meetings.

  - A formal agenda helps keep the meeting on track and assists the SM in focusing on core issues such as revenue generation and staff development.

  - It also ensures that salespeople know what's expected of them so that they'll be prepared to share information as needed.

- **Action:** Create team and individual dashboards or scorecards to track the success of sales and marketing activities.

  - These tools can help the SM evaluate the performance of both individual salespeople and the team, pinpointing needed areas of improvement.

  - Scorecards can also provide information for quickly updating other managers about the sales team's current performance levels.

- **Action:** Analyze sales pipelines to ensure that the levels of sales activity is sufficient to achieve future quotas.

  - The SM should measure the existing dollar value of pipelines levels at each sales stage and in each future monthly sales period, then compare that to the pipeline dollar values required to exceed future actual quotas.

  - By understanding pipeline management, the SM can provide accurate cash-flow and receivables forecasts to the management team.

- **Action:** Run an annual sales-trip contest and quarterly sales games to spotlight team activity. Create clearly defined rules and tracking systems for each contest.

  - Sales contests offer a way for the SM to create a culture that combines fun, performance recognition and competition—while, at the same time, keeping the sales team focused on shared objectives.

- **Action:** Meet with clients regularly to review their satisfaction with your sales and implementation processes.

  - These meetings allow the SM—and, if appropriate, other executives—to check in with a large percentage of the client base. The SM should meet with key clients three times a year and others less frequently, as needed.

  - Obviously, satisfied clients make sales objectives easier to achieve.

- **Action:** Periodically compile win/loss reports to test sales effectiveness.

  - Contact both existing customers and unsuccessful prospects to find out what worked and what didn't. Seek their input on improving sales approaches, sales processes and the actual products or services being sold.

  - This process also helps sales managers stay on top of competitive threats, changing markets and the type of training that salespeople need most.

- **Action:** Determine the appropriate market/territory coverage strategy—defined, open, mixed, account driven.

  - This step allows the SM to assess staffing requirements and sales-organizational designs. It can also assist in market-segmentation strategies.

  - Considering a variety of sales-coverage strategies lets the SM evaluate cost of sales, designs for marketing programs and ratios of market penetration.

- **Action:** Bring compensation plans into alignment with corporate strategies and objectives.

  - The SM must ensure that sales compensation is effectively tracked, that the accounting department prepares compensation-reconciliation statements and that those statements are accurate.

  - Make this assessment quarterly. Ensure that sales activities and compensation models complement the organization's overall strategies and goals. Work to remove any barrier preventing salespeople from hitting those objectives--and doing so on time.

  - Ultimately, the SM must understand and oversee compensation-plan to make sure that it's driving the desired activity and results.

Recruitment

Purpose: The sales manager's most critical function is making sure the sales teams are staffed with high-quality talent. Recruiting should be an ongoing effort. Remember: The best salespeople may not be actively seeking a job just when you happen to have a job opening.

- **Action:** Create an active, ongoing recruiting campaign using a variety of resources. Run ads in the business section of the newspaper and on appropriate job websites. Post a job at least once every 60 days and conduct interviews regularly, even when you don't have specific vacancies.

  - Top-performing sales managers place high priority on finding and retaining top salespeople--and refusing to live with weak talent. Often, sales managers retain salespeople too long either because they feel they've invested too much to let them go or because there's no replacement readily available.

- Another reason that sales managers should focusing on finding and developing great sales talent: Having a high-quality sales team makes their own lives easier!

- **Action:** Use Acumen tools and assessments to create an effective interviewing process that involves at least three other people at your company (for information on Acumen tools, visit www.acumenmgmt.com./ seminars2.phtml).

  - Sales managers should follow a well-defined interviewing process for the same reasons they follow a well-defined sales process: Skipping key steps can lead to big mistakes. In fact, making a bad hire is the most expensive mistake that an SM can make.

  - By involving other colleagues in the hiring process, the SM can consider other viewpoints about particular candidates — which increases the chances of making the right hire.

- **Action:** Network with vendors and others in the industry who can help you find quality candidates.

  - Use conferences, industry events and vendor meetings to help further your search for talent.

Management Communication

Purpose: Management must be kept informed of plans, actions and potential issues at all times. Communication can resolve or prevent all types of political and other challenges that sales managers face each day. A recurring task schedule in Outlook can help ensure regular communication — by regular face-to-face meetings, if possible.

- **Action:** Prepare weekly sales/marketing plans and results to review with other members of the management team.

  - This step helps sales managers build respect with other management-team members. It also opens the door for discussions about how those other managers might assist the sales team in exceeding targets.

  - Frequent communications between the SM and other managers can help increase the management team's trust and confidence in the sales team.

- **Action:** Meet weekly with department heads whose activities impact sales delivery.

  - These meetings can help the SM build rapport with key individuals whose cooperation might assist the sales team. The gatherings can help ensure that monthly and quarterly quotas are attained and help the SM shift resources as necessary to achieve goals.

- **Action:** Prepare rolling six- and 12-month sales plans and communicate at monthly and quarterly meetings.

  - Rolling sales and marketing plans help ensure that the team attains predictable revenue, evening out the peaks and valleys.

  - This action by the SM assists in long-range planning and documents the sales-team's needs.

- **Action:** Focus communications and actions on removing any barriers to a creating sales-driven culture.

- Sales barriers, such dealing with an excessive number of sales documents or having too many people involved in proposal development, can limit the organization's ability to achieve its sales objectives.

- **Action:** Make recommendations to management for new business growth.

  - Sales managers are well-positioned to make such recommendations because of their intimate knowledge of customer needs. Sales managers are on the forefront of customer ideas and market conditions, and their ideas can help keep product and service offerings fresh and competitive.

- **Action:** Make recommendations to management on salesperson terminations.

  - Sales managers must be proactive in developing exactly the right sales team and organization environment.

- **Action:** Schedule regular, formal meetings with the company president.

  - Meet with the chief executive weekly, if possible, to ensure that sales team activity is properly aligned with company priorities.

  - Meet quarterly with the chief executive to review activities and plan for the future.

Acumen

Management Group, Ltd.

Building organizations
through the execution of
strategic sales management

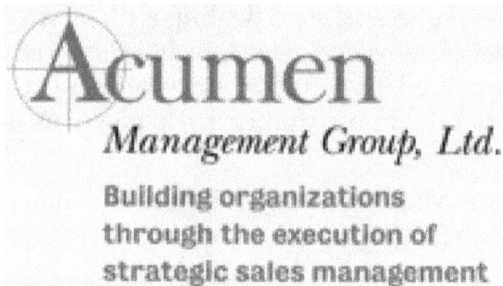

Contact Ken Thoreson

165 Golanvyi Trail, Vonore, TN 37885

(423) 884-6328

Website: www.AcumenManagement.com

Email: Ken@AcumenMgmt.com

Blog: www.YourSalesManagementGuru.com

**Purchase the entire Your Sales Management Guru's
Guide Series at:**

http://YourSalesManagementGuru.SalesGravy.com

About the Author

Ken Thoreson, Acumen Management Group, Ltd. president, is a sales leadership professional who "operationalizes" sales management systems and processes to pull sales results out of the doldrums into the fresh zone of predictable revenue. The sales management thought leader is recognized as an expert in sales execution, channel management, revenue generation, sales analysis, compensation, forecasting, recruitment, and training within the sales function. Over the past 12 years, his consulting, advisory, and platform services have illuminated, motivated, and rejuvenated the sales efforts for companies throughout North America—from emerging , transitional to high-growth. Prior to founding Acumen, he led development-stage, entrepreneurial, and $250-million national vertical software sales organizations as vice president of sales.

As a speaker, Ken energizes audiences and recharges their personal commitment to professional excellence to help drive personal and organizational change and growth. He is a member of The National Speakers Association.

In addition to the two books he has authored and the Sales Management Guru series, Ken's many articles and nationally recognized blog are excellent resources for executives who want to revitalize their organizations. He has been published in Selling Power, VARBusiness, Reseller Management, Business Products Professional and SmartReseller. He is currently a columnist for Redmond Channel Partner Magazine, a publication for Microsoft channel partners.